REMEMBERING

TO FORGIVE

A Tribute to Una O'Higgins O'Malley

Edited by Enda McDonagh

VERITAS

First published 2007 by
Veritas Publications
7/8 Lower Abbey Street
Dublin 1
Ireland
Email publications@veritas.ie
Website www.veritas.ie

Second edition published 2008

ISBN 978 1 84730 156 7

Copyright © The editor and the individual contributors, 2007

10 9 8 7 6 5 4 3 2

'Una' (p. 13), 'Forgiveness' (p. 113) and 'Resurrection' (p. 160) by Padraig J. Daly, cour-
tesy of the author. 'Memory' by Michael D. Higgins (p. 19) courtesy of the author.
'Wounds' (p. 45), 'All of These People' (p. 135) and 'Ceasefire' (p. 156) by Michael
Longley taken from *Collected Poems,* published by Jonathan Cape. Reprinted by permis-
sion of The Random House Group Ltd. 'In Time of War XIX' by W.H. Auden (p. 90)
taken from Edward Mendelson (ed.), *The English Auden: Poems, Essays and Dramatic
Writings 1927–1939*, New York, Random House, pp. 258–9. Line from Brendan
Kennelly's 'Begin' (p. 121) taken from *Selected Poems,* courtesy of E.P. Dutton and
Company Inc., 1972.

Cover image: *Return of the Prodigal Son,* c.1668–69 (oil on canvas) by Rembrandt
Harmensz. van Rijn (1606–69) © Hermitage, St Petersburg, Russia/The Bridgeman Art
Library Nationality/copyright status: Dutch/out of copyright.

A catalogue record for this book is available from the British Library.

Printed in the Republic of Ireland by Betaprint, Dublin

Veritas books are printed on paper made from the wood pulp of managed forests. For
every tree felled, at least one tree is planted, thereby renewing natural resources.

Contents

PART III: FORGIVING

PART IV: RECREATING

Contributors

Padraig J. Daly was born in Dungarven, Co. Waterford in 1943. He is an Augustinian priest and poet, an RTÉ Radio broadcaster and a translator. He has published several collections of poetry, including *The Last Dreamers: New & Selected Poems* (Dedalus Press, 1999) and *The Other Sea* (Dedalus Press, 2003).

Noel Dorr has had a long and distinguished career in the Department of Foreign Affairs. He has held the following positions: Permanent Representative to UN, New York 1980; Irish Representative on UN Security Council 1981–1982; and Secretary General, Department of Foreign Affairs, Dublin, 1987–1995. He is currently Chair of NUI Galway's Údarás na hOllscoile (Governing Authority).

Sean Farren worked as a teacher in Dublin, Switzerland and Sierra Leone before becoming a lecturer at the University of Ulster. In 1982 he was elected to the Northern Ireland Assembly for North Antrim as a member of the SDLP, and was elected again in 1996, 1998 and 2003, during which tenures he held the positions of Minister for Finance and Personnel and Minister of Higher and Further Education, Training and Employment.

Garret FitzGerald was the seventh Taoiseach of Ireland, serving two terms in office. He also served as Foreign Affairs Minister from 1973–1977 and as leader of Fine Gael, 1977–1987. At present FitzGerald is the Chancellor of the National University of Ireland, and President of the Institute of European Affairs.

Brian Garrett is a practising lawyer and arbitrator. He is former Chairman of the Northern Ireland Labour Party and was President of the Irish Association, 1986–1988.

Michael D. Higgins was first elected to Dáil Éireann in the 1981 General Election as a Labour Party TD and has twice served as Mayor of Galway. Higgins has campaigned for human rights, and in recognition of his work he became the first recipient of the Seán MacBride Peace Prize. Michael D. Higgins has also had a career as a poet, author and broadcaster.

Linda Hogan is Professor of Ecumenics at the Irish School of Ecumenics, Trinity College Dublin, teaching a range of courses including Ethics in International Affairs and The Ethics of Human Rights. She is the author of *Confronting the Truth: Conscience in the Catholic Tradition* (Paulist Press, 2000) and *From Women's Experience to Feminist Theology* (Sheffield Academic Press, 1995, 1998).

Dennis Kennedy was born in Co. Antrim in 1936. He worked in the news media in the United States and in Ethiopia before returning to Ireland in 1968 and joining *The Irish Times*. In 1985 he joined the staff of the European Commission where he served as head of its Northern Ireland office until 1991. He now lectures in the Institute of European Studies at Queen's University, Belfast. Publications include *The Widening Gulf* (Blackstaff Press, 1988) and *Living with the European Union: The Northern Ireland Experience* (Macmillan, 2000).

Colum Kenny of the School of Communications, Dublin City University, is a honorary life member of the Glencree Centre for Peace and Reconciliation. His most recent book, *Moments That Changed Us* (Gill and Macmillan, 2005), is a review of Ireland since 1975.

Michael Longley was born in Belfast in 1939 and educated at the Royal Belfast Academical Institution. After reading Classics at Trinity College, Dublin, he taught in schools in Belfast, Dublin and London. He was awarded the Queen's Gold Medal for Poetry in 2001. His most recent publications include *Snow Water* (Jonathan Cape, 2004) and *Collected Poems* (Jonathan Cape, 2006).

Enda McDonagh has been a professor at various universities in Europe and the US. He has authored fifteen books and edited and co-authored sixteen others. He gained his doctorate from the Pontifical University, Maynooth and DCL from the Ludwig-Maximilians Universität, Munich. He was Professor of Moral Theology from 1958–1995 at the Pontifical University, Maynooth, Co. Kildare and Chair of the Governing Body of the University of Cork from 1995–2007. His most recent publication is *Immersed in Mystery: En Route to Theology* (Veritas, 2007).

Dervla Murphy was born in Lismore, Co. Waterford. Since 1964 she has been regularly publishing descriptions of her journeys – by bicycle or on foot – in the more remote areas of four continents. She has also written on the hazards of nuclear power and race relations in Britain. A recent publication is *Eight Feet in the Andes: Travels with a Mule in Unknown Peru* (John Murray, 2006).

Kevin O'Higgins was born in 1946. He was awarded a BA from the National University of Ireland in 1965; called to the Bar in 1968; called to the Inner Bar in 1982; appointed Judge of the Circuit Court in 1986; and appointed Judge of the High Court in 1997. His uncle was Kevin O'Higgins and the late Una O'Higgins O'Malley was his godmother.

Kevin O'Malley is the eldest son of the late Una O'Higgins O'Malley and the late Eoin O'Malley and is a Consultant Surgeon at Dublin's Mater Misericordiae Hospital. He is Chairman of the Medical Board and is a Council Member of the Royal College of Surgeons in Ireland. He is married with four children.

Frank Purcell came to Ireland as a member of the governing body of St Columban's Missionary Society in 1970. He became the Organising Secretary for the Working for Peace group which established the Glencree Centre for Peace and Reconciliation. After his return to Australia in 1976, he was laicised and married. Currently he is involved with the local Interfaith Network and is a member of the Shepparton (Aboriginal) Reconciliation Group.

Mary Robinson first rose to prominence as an academic, barrister, campaigner and member of the Irish Senad. In 1990 she became the first female President of the Republic of Ireland, and served in this role until 1997, whereupon she took up the position of UN High Commissioner for Human Rights (1997–2002). Among many other positions, Robinson has been Honorary President of Oxfam International since 2002; she is Chair of the International Institute for Environment and Development and is also a founding member and Chair of the Council of Women World Leaders.

Geraldine Smyth OP is a Senior Lecturer at the Irish School of Ecumenics, Trinity College Dublin. Her research interests range across the fields of faith and politics, ecclesiology and ethics, and currently, topics on ecumenical reconciliation and the healing of memories. She is engaged in international academic, ecumenical and NGO alliances concerned with transitional justice peacebuilding. Her publications include *The Critical Spirit: Theology at the Crossroads of Faith and Culture – Essays in Honour of Gabriel Daly*, co-edited with Andrew Pierce (Columba, 2003).

Haddon Wilmer is Emeritus Professor of Theology at Leeds University. He entered Cambridge in 1958 after completing national service in the Royal Air Force. He has served as Lecturer, Senior Lecturer and Professor of Theology in the Department of Theology and Religious Studies at the University of Leeds. He was a founder member and chair of the British and Irish Association for Mission Studies.

Forgiveness gives memory a future.

Paul Ricoeur

Una

Padraig J. Daly

We drove to the sandy edges of land,
I recall the powdery gold of the dunes,
Screeching birds;
Your beauty, a reed in the tide.

We eat in a pub in the fields.
You took sodabread and tea,
I had bread and fish.

You had come for refuge,
Your trusted props were gone.
Your lover, Christ,
Was blasting you white.

Later,
In a thin wind,
We walked the shore.
The sun poured pure benediction on the water.

Introduction

THIS COLLECTION OF ESSAYS, by a group of distinguished Irish people, from North and South, as well as one Australian peace activist and one English theologian, who have been involved with the causes of forgiveness and reconciliation so persistently and effectively pursued by Una O'Higgins O'Malley over the period of the Irish Troubles, is intended as more than a symbolic tribute to a great Irish and Christian woman, described at her funeral as 'Ireland's Queen of Peace in the twentieth century'. Born six months before the assassination of her father, Kevin O'Higgins, minister of Home Affairs in the newly established government of the Irish Free State, whose own father had also been assassinated, Una found her public voice and vocation with the outbreak of violence in Northern Ireland in the late 1960s and early 1970s. In this volume, politicians and poets, activists and academics, all co-workers with Una in various ways, rehearse issues of religious and political division, of forgiveness and reconciliation, of justice and peace, as they strive to bring a definitive ending to Irish political violence.

Now, late April 2007, some sixteen months after Una's death on 18 December 2005, the agreement between the two largest and for so long bitterly opposed parties in Northern Ireland, the Democratic Unionist Party and Sinn Féin, seems on the edge of producing the long-desired power-sharing executive. Hopes are high among politicians and people and Una would surely have approved. Yet she would always be conscious of the many problems that remain, which have roots in an angry and destructive past, and their fuller hopes in a transforming and reconciling future. It is around the residual resentments of the past in the early 'Remembering' section, in the potential broadening and restructuring of the present and the (im)mediate future of the middle section and with the final forgiveness and reconciliation of the concluding sections that this book is structured, matching Una's ambitions. The contributors to each section are not, of course, to be narrowly interpreted. They were alive to all dimensions of the problem as laid out here. And they made their mark in that often seemingly endless and fruitless political, cultural and religious dialogue that may just now be yielding its richest harvest.

In the course of the preparation of this book, Una's husband, Eoin, died. He was to have written a foreword. Although a commanding figure in his own surgical field, he was very much a backroom boy, but an extremely effective one, in Una's public campaigns for peace and reconciliation. It was no doubt an extra source of energy in their working together that their two families came from different sides in the Irish civil war and even that their names suggest a merging of Gael (O'Malley) and Viking (O'Higgins). As they belonged together in a turbulent and divided world, we pray they may now enjoy together the peace they longed for in this life.

Enda McDonagh
April 2007

PART I
REMEMBERING

Memory

Michael D. Higgins

'And as Ricoeur said,
To be removed from memory
Is to die twice.'
Nor should it be allowed
To make an amnesia
Of violence.
An amnesty is enough
For the detail.
And who knows whether,
If in time,
Such a healing is possible
As would make an evening
Of forgiveness
Worth the going on.
We make an affirmation.
The stuff of hope beckons.
Out of the darkness
We step,
And blink into the new light.

Sharing Una's Journey

Frank Purcell

> I think in the end we have to accept that our tragedy lies
> always in our past, that we have to live with our ancestors'
> folly and suffer for it, just as they, in their turn, suffered, and
> as we, through our vanity and arrogance, ensure the pain and
> suffering of our children. How to correct history, that's the
> thing.[1]

IT WAS MY PRIVILEGE to share in Una's journey of reconciliation and
forgiveness for three short years, 1972–1975, although for the next thirty
years we shared a correspondence in which she gave a remarkable
commentary on what was happening in Ireland. With hindsight, it was
also the beginning of a personal spiritual journey that Una challenged me
to take. Her challenge was not given in words but in the example of her
own willingness both to ask for and to offer forgiveness for the heartaches,
the injustices, the hatreds that flared anew in Ireland in the late 1960s.
Una was ever-conscious of the fact that her own father was the cause of
pain and heartache for some families of his generation. She, in turn,
suffered the pain of loss of the assassinated father she was too young to
remember and an assassinated grandfather. From that experience grew
Una's deep empathy for those who had suffered or were suffering such
losses – be they the children of the civil war or the new victims, Catholic
and Protestant, in the North.

Coming to Ireland as an Australian priest in 1970 was for me to enter a
world at once so familiar and yet so puzzling. It was Celtic and yet even

the graduates of a basic national school education could quote Shakespeare and English poetry at length while in the midst of a political discussion on 'perfidious Albion'. I had no sense of the debt of pain and suffering which had to be paid to win independence from Britain. Nor had I any appreciation of the pain and anger that still existed fifty years or so after the bloody civil war that accompanied the birth of the Irish state. But I still sensed something extraordinary was happening one night at an ecumenical service that Una organised in the Leeson Park Church in Dublin. Children of a number of the main protagonists of the civil war gathered in that Protestant church to pray together. President Childers, a Protestant, was there, as were Garrett FitzGerald, Liam Cosgrove, and Una O'Malley, the daughter of Kevin O'Higgins. And just as the service was about to begin, the former president, de Valera himself, came into the church. It was then that I realised what Una was on about. She was trying to show that reconciliation was possible and that there could be peace and harmony on the island. It was a sacramental occasion – it was both a sign of reconciliation and an occasion of grace. It was an event that signalled that it is possible to be reconciled in spite of injustices, brutality, hatred and fear. But the way forward requires love of even our enemies, that love which Christ has taught as the key to his kingdom. There is no resolution unless the perpetrator has the humility to listen to the cries of the victim and acknowledge the injustices inflicted on the other. There can be no reconciliation unless the perpetrators seek the forgiveness of the victims and no peace and harmony unless the victims are able to accept those apologies and forgive their persecutors. That ceremony organised by Una was sacramental in the sense that it was not only a sign of what could be, but also a means through which the gift and strength of Christ's love poured into our hearts that night. That was the insight which Una had drawn from her own father's dying example, as well as that of her Saviour.

Part of the tragedy of those years was the failure to believe that non-violent political remedies could deliver a solution. The extraordinary resolution of the Civil War in Ireland, where an unarmed police force gained the confidence of the people on both sides, where the victors in that armed struggle were able to hand over political power to their opponents within a few short years, where the rule of law, parliamentary democracy and political accountability flourished in a situation of high unemployment, poverty and emigration, all offered an example which too few at that time saw and believed in. Yet by the 1970s, the first stirrings of the Celtic Tiger were beginning to show the potential of a poor but educated people skilled in the arts of democratic politics. The real tragedy for Northern Ireland was the recourse to arms by the IRA at a time when globalisation and the entry of Britain and Ireland into the European Union offered powerful non-violent alternatives. Taking up arms, initially to defend themselves against the thuggery and bullying of the Loyalist paramilitaries and the mindless savagery of the paratroopers in Derry was understandable, but a tragedy. Looking back over the past forty years, it is now clear that we were seeing the death throes of colonialism. Ireland didn't need a final dose of violence.

The carnage and chaos in Iraq today is a reminder of what happens when the violent option is chosen as the way to change society. The alternative, a non-violent political option, was well worth a try in Northern Ireland in the late 1960s and early 1970s. If the political, diplomatic and economic power of Western democracies together with the moral authority of the United Nations had been brought to bear, Britain would have been under enormous pressure to seek solutions that respected the hopes and fears of both sides. Britain got off the hook because of the violence that made the British Army appear to be defenders of the innocent. The ambivalence of its role was hidden by the fear of paramilitary terror on the streets. With the violent option taken by both sides, the cycle of fear, violence, death, grieving and loss spread through the country. A small number of people like Una struggled to offer an alternative. They knew that there had to be a solution to the long unresolved grievances of the Catholics in the North. There also had to be reassurances for the many Protestants in those same counties who feared the loss of their religious and personal identity and of their culture under a united Ireland where they would be subject to the 'tyranny of a Catholic majority'. People in the Republic knew that their contribution to a resolution would always be secondary to that of those engaged in the challenge in the North. The challenge for Una and her fellow members in

Working for Peace and similar organisations in the Republic was to identify issues that had an all-Ireland dimension and could be tackled legitimately in the Republic. That was their goal. They began by offering temporary refuge and respite for victims of the disturbances in Belfast. But soon they began to tackle the underlying obstacles to peace and harmony in Ireland. The ecumenical service in Leeson Park Church was one of their first steps in taking up that task.

At that time in Ireland, the presence of the Apostolic Nuncio at an ecumenical service in a Protestant church was a major statement from the Vatican. It was signalling the importance of inter-faith dialogue. Unfortunately, it was a lesson that the Irish Catholic bishops at the time seemed to miss. My impression of those bishops in the early 1970s was that they were not convinced that the Vatican Council's calls for renewal were all that relevant for the Irish Church. After all, most of the population went to Mass on Sunday, got married in the Church and had their children baptised. Any excess energy for the Church was being expended in the mission world, where Irish priests and nuns in their thousands were a major source of personnel in Africa, Asia and Latin America. What more needed to be done? The bishops as a group hadn't begun to face up to the implications of Vatican II for the Church's understanding of its mission. Mission was no longer seen as something the Church did in the Third World. It was to apply across the First World as well. The mission was to build the Kingdom of God – to transform our personal lives as well as the social, cultural, political and economic relationships that make up the cultures and the kind of world in which we live today. Much of that mission is the responsibility of the laity, drawing on the moral principles of Christ and the Church, as well as on their own experience and practical know-how. While it is not the bishops' role to come up with political solutions, bishops and priests do have a major role in supporting and encouraging the laity. Unfortunately, in the early 1970s there was little public committment by bishops and priests to the alternative options of non-violence and reconciliation.

Una, among others, played an important part in exercising an informal Christian leadership that was in stark contrast to the lack of strong leadership and courage within the official ranks. A few Catholic priests had acknowledged that Church renewal had a role to play. They recognised that the perception of Catholicism practised in Ireland had played a role in maintaining fear and sectarianism among many of the Protestants in the North. They could see the deepening alienation caused by the increasing use of violence by Republicans in order to further their aims. But these priests were not popular with their bishops – and often not too popular with their fellow priests. The seminary formation of that time had turned out all too many timid and cautious men. They were as unwilling to take a strong stand against violence being used by Catholics as they were unwilling to even test the impact that integrated Protestant–Catholic schools might have on community relations. They might have preached against violence once in a while, but they were unwilling to enter into serious dialogue with Protestant laity or clergy to explore joint approaches to better social cohesion and community harmony. All too many religious leaders on both sides in those early days were tribal chaplains rather than countercultural prophets of justice, peace and reconciliation. It wasn't that the Catholic bishops didn't condemn violence. They did that after every outrage. But it was as if they didn't see that religion in Ireland was part of the problem. They didn't recognise that the kind of Catholicism and the kind of Protestantism that influenced Irish people, both nationalist and loyalist, were not only part of the problem, but also had to be part of the solution. There could be no solution to the Irish problem without a serious renewal of its Catholicism and Protestantism. This was the insight that drove many members of the Working for Peace group to establish the Glencree Centre for Peace and Reconciliation. They dreamed of it bringing Catholic and Protestant together to build relationships, foster trust and begin dialogue to seek solutions that would mean peace and justice for all. But the need for reform was a delicate issue in Catholic Ireland. Ecumenism wasn't a priority. Nor was there any indication that the bishops saw the Irish conflict as a challenge for the Church itself.

Perhaps partition was partly responsible for this. The Protestant minority in the South became so small subsequent to partition that the

Catholic Church simply didn't see the other churches as either spiritual or political equals, a perception supported by the controversial Art. 44 of the de Valera constitution of 1937. The role of the Catholic Church in the North was different; there they saw themselves servicing an embattled minority in an unfriendly state. The hierarchy is an all-Ireland body, but gave greater priority to preserving its status in the South than to improving relations between Catholics and the northern state. Yet two issues were crying out for reform and renewal in the Catholic Church at the time. One was the problem shared with the theologically conservative Protestant Churches in the North – an exclusivist interpretation of our vocation as God's chosen people. The bishops hadn't begun to spell out the implications of the more inclusive teaching by the Vatican Council of the universality of God's love and compassion. They hadn't begun to reinterpret the call to be God's chosen people as a call to mission – a calling to be a member of a community whose witness of faith, service and love for all people, in word and Christ-like action, would make Jesus present to people today. Instead they allowed the traditional exclusive interpretation of 'no salvation outside the Church' to remain unchallenged. The bishops took no strong lead in acknowledging that the Spirit of Jesus was leading people to faith and love in ways unknown to us. They ignored the role of that exclusivist theology in fuelling division and hatred between Catholic and Protestant. All too many of them saw one another not as brothers and sisters in Christ but as enemies threatening the religious and national identities of one another. The 'others' were the enemy of God and of God-fearing people.

Things did gradually change in Ireland but one can only wonder if the Catholic bishops played a leading role in that development. As late as 1998, the Believers Enquiry Project at Glencree asked the churches in Ireland to respond to the question, 'What is the role of your Church in building peace and who can work with you in that endeavour?' The article notes that the 'major religion of Ireland was not officially represented in the Enquiry'.[2]

By default, the bishops allowed a demonising and scapegoating of the 'others' who were destined inevitably for hell-fire. I still remember as a child in Australia the difficulty the nuns had in our catechism classes when asked about the salvation of non-Catholics. They were uneasy with the theology because they knew that a number of the children had non-Catholic parents. The Australian sensitivity was not obvious in Ireland as I experienced it at that time. Nor was ecumenism high on the Catholic bishops' agenda. By contrast, in spite of the blatantly anti-Catholic preaching of Dr Ian Paisley in Ulster, some significant ecumenical moves were made by the Presbyterian Church in the North before the outbreak of violence in the late 1960s. Fr Ray Davey set up the Corrymeela Community and began to bring Catholic and Protestant together to build bridges of friendship and to initiate the beginnings of dialogue. His efforts had an especial credibility because they had begun before the outbreak of violence in the late 1960s.

But there was another significant factor behind the Catholic bishops' lack of enthusiasm for ecumenism and the need for renewal. There was something deeper that has only surfaced clearly since the 'outing' of paedophilia among some of the clergy in the English-speaking world. All too often, the protection of the institution rather than the needs and rights of the victims was given priority by our bishops. The damage to the credibility of the Catholic Church caused by that un-Christian priority will take generations to repair. So when I first came into contact with Una, the exclusivist theology so widespread in Ireland and the bishops' practical commitment to protect the institutional dimension of the Church at all costs were unacknowledged but significant elements in the Irish problem. The bishops failed to recognise or acknowledge that religion was not the innocent victim of cynical manipulation by social, economic and political forces operating outside their control. They failed to recognise at the time that it was very much part of the problem. It was as if they instinctively knew that any acknowledgement that religion was part of the problem would mean that it had to be part of the solution. And that might weaken their ability to protect the institution and their authority. So when some Catholic laypeople joined forces with Protestants to improve community relationships through an experimental integrated schooling project, they were hit with the full force of episcopal authority. When suggestions for co-education were proposed within the Republic, the Catholic Church only reluctantly agreed to introduce it in rural areas where student numbers demanded a change for the sake of survival. Single sex schools were maintained in the towns and cities where pupil numbers were sufficient to maintain the tradition. The Catholic Church, as institution, opposed any developments that might weaken its control over the education of Catholic children. Priests who tried to do something in cross-community activities also seemed to run into problems with their bishops. A few priests with the backing of their religious orders, particularly the Jesuits and the Redemptorists, did get involved but the main game was taken up by the laity.

On the Catholic side, the laity emerged as the key defenders of the need to rethink our relationships, find non-violent alternatives to the IRA approach and begin tackling the mutual lack of respect for the faith traditions of the other. They faced up to the sectarianism and bitterness that was part of the problem and searched for solutions. Una became an alternative prophetic voice, offering leadership through her public statements and her activities in the search for reconciliation. Her goals were simple. She led the way in urging all the members of the Working for Peace group to show their respect for the other religious denominations represented among their membership. The practical step she offered was to call on Working for Peace members to attend, in turn, the Sunday services of the various religious denominations to be found among its membership. Not many years before, Catholics were unable to attend any services in Protestant churches. Una broke that taboo with other Catholic members of Working for Peace.

Its impact was quite extraordinary. I remember taking an English guest of mine to the local Church of Ireland church one Sunday morning, as he was more comfortable going to a Protestant service. I went in full clericals and stayed till the end. I'll never forget the look of amazement and delight on the face of the rector of that church when I introduced myself afterwards. I would never have done that without Una's example to challenge me. But there was another range of practical steps that Una took to build bridges of trust in preparation for real dialogue. There were

27

meetings with Ian Paisley at Stormont, with Sinn Féin leaders at their Kevin Street headquarters, with the English ambassador and his staff in Dublin, visits to Belfast and Corrymeela, to Kennedy connections in Boston, Pittsburgh and Washington. She even made it to the Pope himself. In many ways she reminds me of that great model of Catholic womanhood whom the current Pope Benedict has held up as a model for apostolic women – St Catherine of Siena. She too took action when the official leadership of the Church was paralysed with inaction during the exile of the papacy in Avignon.

Una was a Vatican II Catholic. She knew that it wasn't bishops and priests who had to carry out the mission of the Church. It is the laity who have to do it. It is their example, their commitment to public life and their practical application of Christ's spirit in the way they live their lives in collaboration with all people of good will, religious and secular, that can transform society and make it a place of justice, peace and harmony. It was Una's conviction that religion had the potential to assist the process of reconciliation through respecting religious freedom, acknowledging God's spirit at work in 'others' and recognising the damage that our attitude to 'others' could and had caused. She also knew that religion had the potential to fuel hatred and violence and could allow itself to be manipulated for social, economic and political agendas. Church renewal and ecumenism were essential to avoid that and enable religion to be part of the solution to the Irish problem. That was her dream and she spent thirty years trying to make it a reality. Her husband Eoin and her family supported her in that and made it possible for her to take that journey.

Notes

1   Robert Fisk, *The Great War for Civilisation: The Conquest of the Middle East*, New York, Vintage, 2007, p. 1283.
2   Mairin Colleary, in Colin Murphy and Lynne Adair (eds), *A Place for Peace, Glencree Centre for Reconciliation, 1974–2004*, Dublin, The Liffey Press, 2004, p. 14.

The Way We Were

Brian Garrett

EVERYONE WHO KNEW Una O'Higgins O'Malley quickly recognised how troubled she was by the events that occurred in Northern Ireland from August 1969 onwards and how strong her opposition was to the sectarian violence unleashed by the IRA and mirrored by loyalist groups. Her views were never those of a detached observer. Una's generally irenic demeanour, which characterised her personality, never prevented her expression of deep antagonism towards these events. It was natural that Una should have become a founding figure of the Centre for Peace and Reconciliation at Glencree, and during her presidency of the Irish Association (1984–1986) she would build contacts throughout Ireland (and, tellingly, various contacts with individuals and groups of the unionist tradition in Northern Ireland).

Today this type of example displayed by Una is more widely respected. It is right to recall, however, that in the 1970s and 1980s (indeed somewhat later) it was less than universally admired, so that many who shared Una's views frequently found themselves criticised as being somehow less than truly Irish; one needs only to examine the many newspaper columns and streams of letters to newspaper editors in this vein and recall how widely this criticism circulated in nationalist Ireland, north and south. While Una's was not a lone voice, she willingly accepted the risk of being classified as someone betraying her roots. There were others in Ireland who, like Una, consistently argued the case for greater understanding and denounced those who supported, or were ambivalent about, the IRA campaign, and these individuals also included those whose family background, as in Una's case, was one of involvement in earlier pivotal political events in Ireland, such as 1916 Rising, the War of Independence or the Irish Civil War. Criticism of the IRA campaign from this source was telling and here mention might be made of similar contributions by other members of the Irish Association, including Garret FitzGerald and Ruairi and Maire Brugha (nee MacSwiney). Of note too was Conor Cruise O'Brien's sustained and trenchant criticism of republicanism and those who displayed a tendency to seek the cover of the ethnic penumbra which the IRA so assiduously created. These individuals provided reassurance that the incipient civil war would not materialise and, despite ambivalence in some quarters, the overwhelming body of opinion in Ireland did not support the IRA campaign of violence.

An explanation of my connection with Una is relevant. This came about principally through our shared membership of the Irish Association where, in 1986, I succeeded her as president. We had also both participated in a protest picket in 1972 outside Provisional Sinn Féin headquarters in Kevin Street, Dublin – an occasion which I have particular reason to recall as on returning to Belfast at the end of that demonstration I found that my office, along with others, had suffered severe bomb damage as a result of another IRA bombing in the city centre. It fell principally to Una during her presidency of the Irish Association to promote a sustained North/South dialogue at a level not achieved during the Association's previous twenty-year history. The Irish Association, no doubt anxious to ensure that offence was not given to its members who came from both parts of Ireland and from different political traditions, had striven in general to steer clear of more controversial political issues. Not so under Una's leadership and I found myself swept along in full agreement with her view that if violence and conflict were so obviously raging outside then those disturbing events must be faced squarely at Association meetings. In retrospect, I am sure I overlooked the fact that the post-1969 Troubles must have caused a considerable deal of personal agony for Una whose father, Kevin O'Higgins, had been such an important figure in the first Irish government after partition and who, when Una was less than six months old, was notoriously murdered in

1927 by fratricidal republicans while on his way to Mass in south Dublin. As *The Times* obituary observed:

> She did not allow the deep hurt she felt at never knowing the father whose memory she revered to deteriorate into bitterness but used it as a springboard for a commitment to forgiveness and reconciliation. She found inspiration in her father's journey from a republican revolutionary to espousing proposals to crown George V King of Ireland in Dublin if Northern Ireland agreed to unite with the Irish Free State.

Before turning to some personal doubts on features of the Belfast (Good Friday) Agreement I am also reminded that Una during her presidency opposed the idea that the Irish Association should declare itself in support of the 1985 Anglo-Irish Agreement concluded at Hillsborough, Co. Down, which was later to provide part of the framework on which the Belfast Agreement was constructed. The overwhelming response of Irish Association members to the 1985 Hillsborough Agreement was clearly one of support but, as Una argued, to proceed at that time to nail the Association's colours to the Hillsborough mast risked excluding a body of (unionist) opinion which was then strongly opposed to the Hillsborough Agreement. Una's decision in this context proved wise even if it did not reflect her personal view which favoured the Agreement.

The passage of more than eight years since the 1995 Belfast Agreement was concluded provides a basis here to reflect on its impact on political life in Northern Ireland and to consider its likely longer term effect on voting attitudes in Northern Ireland. The comments which now follow, however, are not presented as either a comprehensive overview or a certain prediction.

In 1998, along with the majority within each of the two main communities in Northern Ireland, I voted in support of the Belfast Agreement and, like many others, I hoped it would mark the end of terrorist violence (and acceptance on all sides that weapons must be given up speedily) and provide a firm basis for a new start when both communities could be expected to work together in common cause. The much quoted line of Seamus Heaney of how hope and history might rhyme seemed apt, even if there was reason to place a good deal more weight on the hope as opposed to the history side of his poetic equation.

In Northern Ireland 953,583 people (81 per cent of the Northern Ireland electorate) voted in the referendum on the Belfast Agreement and of this number 676,966 (71.12 per cent) voted in favour with 274,879 (28.88 per cent) against. The question that had been posed in Northern Ireland was framed as a simple choice, viz 'Do you support the agreement reached in the multi-party talks on Northern Ireland and set out in Command Paper 3883?' The resulting 'Yes' vote in the referendum in Northern Ireland is understood to have comprised a majority of voters within each of the two main religious/political communities even if the Protestant/unionist community vote suggested a relatively close split. Whatever else, this endorsement of the Belfast Agreement undoubtedly provided necessary legitimacy for the new arrangements.

In turn the electorate in the Republic of Ireland overwhelmingly endorsed approval of changes in the Irish Constitution (Articles 2 and 3) on which result the Belfast Agreement had also been posited. These new articles were devised to abandon the earlier de jure (albeit suspended) claim of sovereignty over Northern Ireland without at the same time deserting those who might cherish belief in Irish nationhood or wished to enjoy Irish citizenship. Thus the new Articles 2 and 3:

Article 2

It is the entitlement and birthright of every person born in the island of Ireland, which includes its islands and seas, to be part of the Irish nation. That is also the entitlement of all persons otherwise qualified in accordance with law to be citizens of Ireland. Furthermore, the Irish nation cherishes its special affinity with people of Irish ancestry living abroad who share its cultural identity and heritage.

Article 3

1. It is the firm will of the Irish nation, in harmony and friendship, to unite all the people who share the territory of the island of Ireland, in all the diversity of their identities and traditions, recognising that a united Ireland shall be brought about only by peaceful means in both jurisdictions with the consent of a majority of the people, democratically expressed, in both jurisdictions in the island. Until then, the laws enacted by the Parliament established by this Constitution shall have the like area and extent of application as the laws enacted by the Parliament that existed immediately before the coming into operation of this Constitution.

With the outcome of the referendums the stage appeared set for the old order of things, so far as relations between the two communities in Northern Ireland were concerned, to be transformed and relations normalised between the two parts of Ireland. What has followed has not always been so reassuring on the inter-community front although the inter-Ireland formula has been highly successful.

It is not possible to rehearse here all the events that occurred between April 1998 and the date when this contribution was prepared but it may be worth recalling that this period saw the collapse of the Northern Ireland Executive on three occasions, the voice of both moderate unionism and nationalism being increasingly disregarded, as well as marked electoral drift towards the ultra politics represented respectively by DUP and Sinn Féin. Many explanations are tendered for these developments, including the durability of long nurtured inter-community distrust against a background of continuing (if decreasing) paramilitary activity culminating in the Omagh bombing carried out by dissent republican elements. So far as the stance of the British and Irish governments were concerned throughout the period, this increasingly assumed 'Puss-in-Boots' look combined with what seemed the policy of giving preference to the demands of the DUP and Sinn Féin.

The question which might be posed is whether there is at the heart of the Belfast Agreement a contradiction that will block the achievement of greater inter-community inclusiveness and buttress sectarianism. At the time of this contribution the timetable for devolution in Northern Ireland set by the British government is running out and it is as yet uncertain whether devolution will be achieved despite the measure of agreement that appears to have been obtained during discussions at St Andrews, Scotland, on 20 October 2006 (referred to as the 'St Andrews' Agreement' but the character of this latter 'Agreement' is limited to being that of an agreed statement by the two governments).

What then can be shown to be a cause for anxiety for those who wish for greater inter-community harmony? It is true that the biggest problem is that of the strength of the enduring quality of historic inter-community antagonism and not the Belfast Agreement itself. But even if one acknowledges this uncomfortable fact, consideration should be given to the question of whether the Belfast Agreement will strengthen sectarian structures.

In an article in *Fortnight* (October 2006) Peter Shirlow and Brendan Murtagh argued that the Agreement has increased sectarian attitudes and behaviour. The authors observed:

> In certain ways the Agreement validated the importance of competing identities through wrongly acknowledging ethno-sectarian blocs as benign 'traditions'. The masking of ethno-sectarian competition as 'tradition' presented alternative and invalid cultural position as both feasible and correct.

It is not however all one-way traffic. The Belfast Agreement has provided a formula for inter-party government and placed valuable emphasis on the 'equality agenda'. Against this there can be little doubt that the formula used to construct any incoming Northern Ireland Executive is little less than an open invitation to the electorate to resort to a traditional sectarian headcount so that electors can then hardly be blamed if they believe their immediate community interest (in terms of the composition of the

Northern Ireland Executive under the d'Hondt system of proportionality to electoral seats won) will be most conveniently secured by voting on traditional lines (Protestant/Unionist – Catholic/Nationalist/Republican). This invitation inevitably underpins the appeal of the main community ultra political parties in each community (DUP and Sinn Féin). Not surprisingly then that the Northern Ireland Assembly procedure includes a requirement that those elected must register a designation of their political identity (confined to 'nationalist, unionist or other') with this in turn used as the means to measure cross-community support for certain more controversial Northern Ireland Assembly votes. Of interest in this last context is a paragraph found at Annex A to the St Andrews' Agreement which suggests that this community designation procedure might be further copper-fastened. Article 15 of Annex A states:

> An amendment to the 1998 Act would provide that an Assembly Member would not be able to change community designation for the whole of the Assembly term except in the case of a change of membership of political party.

Nice work if you can get it, or nice, that is, for confessional political parties. Nor should it be overlooked that these arrangements have been set in a framework which effectively rules out any practical prospect of opposition politics within the Northern Ireland Assembly.

The Pledge of Office for ministers under the Belfast Agreement is as follows:

(a)   To discharge in good faith all the duties of office;
(b)   commitment to non-violence and exclusively peaceful and democratic means;
(c)   to serve all the people of Northern Ireland equally, and to act in accordance with the general obligations on government to promote equality and prevent discrimination;
(d)   to participate with colleagues in the preparation of a programme for government;

(e)   to operate within the framework of that programme when agreed within the Executive Committee and endorsed by the Assembly;

(f)   to support, and to act in accordance with, all decisions of the Executive Committee and Assembly;

(g)   to comply with the Ministerial Code of Conduct.

This Pledge of Office contains much to commend it, not least the provision in sub-paragraph (c) which specifically requires ministers 'to serve all the people of Northern Ireland equally'. The difficulty, however, is to find anywhere in the Agreement provision that would set as an obligation the need to work for the integration of the two communities. Equality and integration (or social inclusiveness) should be twin goals. In view of the unhappy past of Northern Ireland there would be advantage in bearing in mind the views expounded by the US Supreme Court Justices in the context of segregated schools (in the 1954 decision Brown v Board of Education for Topeka) that 'separate is not necessarily equal'. Equality is most effective if it embraces, wherever practicable, the notion of inclusiveness and is not designed to provide a purely mechanistic basis to prop up community separation. Accordingly, legislative and executive decisions in Northern Ireland might with value be made subject to scrutiny as to their expected effect in promoting inter-community inclusiveness – a test which could be added to that in Section 75 of the Northern Ireland Act which requires public authority decisions etc. to be submitted to equality and non-discrimination tests.

A range of response to any suggestion that the Belfast Agreement should be re-visited can be expected. From outside Northern Ireland one anticipates a measure of exasperation – 'Who cares? We've had enough of that troublesome place' – and this response is understandable in the wider international setting where there are so many greater and pressing problems. Within Britain and Ireland the most likely response would be that it is as yet too early to expect greater things in Northern Ireland and so, rather than risk an acrimonious debate, it would be wiser to let the current arrangements work themselves through over a further, perhaps lengthy, period even if in the interim this may result in some uncomfortable consequences. Nor is the current situation in Northern Ireland all bleak. A number of significant achievements have come about in civic life in Northern Ireland with progress in such areas as equality legislation, police reform and the attainment of a greatly improved workforce balance. Some of these achievements accompanied the Belfast Agreement, although most of the progress in the non-discrimination field pre-dates 1998. There is reason to hope too that such progress as has been made in inter-community terms in Northern Ireland will in time itself set a new agenda and challenge ingrained attitudes; one recent example (and there are others) which gives cause for hope is the creation outside Enniskillen of the first integrated social housing project in Carran Crescent where residents from both communities have signed a neighbourhood charter banning partisan displays etc. In passing it is appropriate to note the continuing success of integrated schools in Northern Ireland – a sector which as yet is relatively small in comparison with the controlled (essentially Protestant) and maintained (Catholic) sectors but it is the integrated sector which is growing at the fastest rate and becoming an increasingly important feature of the schooling system.

So what more could or should be done? The Belfast Agreement contains provision for review (Strand One, Para 36) but this is to be a review designed to deal with procedural rather than framework features and is expressly limited to be 'with a view to agreeing any adjustments necessary in the interests of efficiency and fairness'. At St Andrews the question of review was reduced to the suggestion that an amendment could be introduced permitting the appointment by the Northern Ireland Assembly of a Standing Institutional Review Committee but that this would be expressly confined to 'operational aspects of Strand One institutions'.

If there is to be a wider review then it would need to be carried out without a pre-ordained outcome in mind or one which would tend to distort free elections or discount the rights of the ultra political parties. Any outcome of such a review would also need to be submitted to referendum. In conclusion, the Belfast Agreement would be best not regarded either as unchallengeable Holy Writ nor constantly glossed to the extent that it becomes an unchangeable formula permanently fixed for future generations regardless of consequence. Within the next generation or so there is likely to be reason to revisit the Belfast Agreement – and somehow I am convinced that Una O'Higgins O'Malley would not disagree.

En Route to Partnership

Sean Farren

> We stand, not for the perpetuation of hatred, but for the
> rooting up and elimination of old hatreds, old furies, and the
> quenching of old fires; we stand for peace and sanity and
> construction in this country, and peace between neighbour.

SO SPOKE KEVIN O'HIGGINS during the Dáil debate on the outcome to
the Boundary Commission in 1925. O'Higgins recognised that, while the
Irish struggle for independence that had climaxed four years earlier with
the Anglo-Irish Treaty had brought independence to twenty-six counties,
it would be impossible to extend that independence to embrace all thirty-
two counties without 'the rooting up and elimination of old hatreds, old
furies ...' Una O'Higgins O'Malley profoundly shared her father's
sentiments. Throughout her public life she strove with a single-minded
and creative determination to meet the challenge of achieving the goals
these sentiments imply for relationships between the two main political
traditions on this island: unionism and nationalism. Today the best
prospects for meeting that challenge lie with the Good Friday [Belfast]
Agreement of 1998, now further amplified by the St Andrews' Agreement
of October 2006 and strengthened by the historic developments of March
and May 2007 which made restoration of the North's political institutions
possible. Despite the difficulties of its early years, the Good Friday
Agreement has finally shown itself to offer the best possible basis on which
to resolve the tensions that arise from the diversity of national allegiances,

religious beliefs and political aspirations of the people of Northern Ireland and between the people of Ireland as a whole.

Fundamentally, the agreement commits its signatories to a process of democratic dialogue and political partnership within a constitutional and political framework that respects the identities, aspirations and allegiances of all. The constitutional and institutional provisions of the agreement, together with what are termed its 'confidence building measures' – human rights, policing and judicial reform, prisoner releases, decommissioning of paramilitary arms, cultural rights etc. – addressed all of the contentious issues that lay at the heart of the conflict. In doing so, the agreement became the most comprehensive ever between representatives of the Irish people and between Ireland and Britain. Furthermore, voters North and South in Ireland emphatically endorsed it in the joint referenda of May 1998. Kevin O'Higgins, like his daughter, would have been among those foremost in promoting the agreement. As far as Irish unity is concerned, by asserting that democratic, peaceful persuasion is the only acceptable means of achieving that goal, the agreement rejected the physical force approach long central to so many tragically futile campaigns undertaken in its name. Indeed, difficult as it was to do so in 1925, only four years after Ireland had been partitioned and more than seventy before the Good Friday Agreement was signed, O'Higgins and his colleagues clearly accepted that Northern Ireland would retain its status within the UK unless and until a majority voted for change. Una also voiced the same approach long before the agreement of 1998 and vigorously opposed the campaign of violence which, lacking any political or moral legitimacy and with no hope of success, only continued to stoke 'old hatred [and] old furies'. Effectively, the O'Higgins' position and that of the Good Friday Agreement itself means that Irish unity has to be argued and worked for in terms of what must be demonstrated as in the best interests of all of the people of Ireland, 'Catholic, Protestant and Dissenter', and not merely in terms of what is asserted to be in their interest.

The Good Friday Agreement does not assume that unionists are nationalists in waiting. Much less does it imply that unionists live in a state of false consciousness as to their nationality. Rather, the agreement is a covenant of honour between nationalists and unionists, an agreement whose principles and even some of whose structures can endure, regardless of constitutional change, because they are in the best interest of peace, stability and reconciliation. As such, the agreement enables conflict to be replaced by a peaceful competition of ideas between unionism and nationalism, while also enabling people of both traditions to work together to forge a better society for all. That is what the partnership arrangements for governing Northern Ireland are intended to provide and also what the North–South or all-island elements of the agreement are intended to create. It is within the North that that engagement will obviously be at its most intense because it is there that relationships between unionists and nationalists are most immediate, most acute and most painful. Despite an end to violent conflict, the pain in those relationships persists. It is still deeply felt by those who were affected by loss, by injury or by the destruction of their livelihood as a result of violence. The pain is to be seen in relationships between political parties, in the tensions surrounding parades and in attitudes towards the police. But it persists also in the many unreported minor acts of sectarian-motivated verbal and physical abuse expressed and perpetrated by one side on the other. Regrettably it frequently still manifests itself amongst young people for whom the years of violence are only known through the pages of history books or, more dangerously, through the folklore of their communities.

In many areas children from different schools in the same towns no longer share bus stops or school buses when travelling to and from their schools. School timetables are adjusted so the exodus from one school does not converge with the exodus from another – all to reduce the ever-present possibility of sectarian confrontation. Young people wearing the 'wrong' sporting colours run serious risks of being assaulted if they venture into the 'wrong' neighbourhood. Celebrating a team's victory can provoke a riot if the venue is too near an interface area; buses carrying people to some event or other can be attacked simply by passing close to the 'wrong' ghetto; even city-centre places of entertainment have become marked as 'orange' or 'green'; investments and developments in one community are jealously compared to those in the 'other'.

More significantly, consider the following contrast. Thanks to strong employment legislation, people increasingly work in more religiously integrated workplaces. But at the same time people are increasingly residing in religiously segregated neighbourhoods. Such segregation leads, not surprisingly, to one-sided socialising, reinforces school-based segregation and produces a society in which the 'other side' still remains subject to very negative stereotyping. Past and present insults, injuries and pain are kept fresh as stereotypes are passed intact from one generation to the next. Politically, segregation reinforces solidarity around those parties that portray themselves strongest at standing up to those perceived as a threat on the 'other' side. In practice, it leads to the harassment of minority-group residents and frequently to their involuntary departure from neighbourhoods where they have lived for many years. The outcome is the maintenance of suspicions and antagonisms that feed intercommunal tensions, hatred and conflict. This tension boils over during the marching season, leaving society wondering how and when fundamental change for the better will ever be registered in community relationships.

Yet another paradox is that neither community in the North lacks for initiatives aimed at bringing about that kind of change, initiatives of the kind that Una endorsed. A considerable amount of effort, commitment and organisation is invested in all kinds of programmes aimed at eliminating sectarianism and developing a more respectful approach to community relations within the North and between North and South. And such initiatives have their successes. There is more awareness and more knowledge about and between communities and increasingly more is being undertaken under cross-community and all-Ireland auspices. Schools, youth organisations, women's groups, development groups, religious groups, arts groups, sporting groups and many more are engaged in these programmes. If it is difficult to measure the scale of their achievements, one has to wonder how much worse the situation could be if they didn't exist. Certainly the scale on which they exist and the scope of their work must rank amongst the most positive community-based developments of the past twenty-five years.

Overcoming and eliminating such manifestations of sectarian divisions will take time but tackling them in a concerted way is an almost impossible task in the absence of shared political institutions. If political representatives cannot be seen to be cooperating but instead are seen as perpetually at loggerheads, there are no shared examples of how positive relationships can be developed across the North's community divide. People may now enjoy the same rights but without political institutions functioning to provide opportunities for political leaders to be seen working together, there is little or no sense of social cohesion or mutual responsibility. That is why it is critical that political institutions are fully restored and operated in a true spirit of partnership. A cold-war approach filled with mutual suspicion would only undermine the whole thrust towards reconciliation. On the all-Ireland stage, the opportunities created by the Good Friday Agreement to forge economic, social and cultural links by the establishment of the North–South Ministerial Council have marked another sea change for the better. The work of such bodies as Intertrade Ireland, Waterways Ireland, Tourism Ireland and the Languages Body, as well as initiatives in wider fields such as health and education, are evidence of the benefits to be gained by people and communities through cooperation on an all-Ireland basis. The growth in North–South trade, the development of research to business links on an all-island basis, the development of a single-island tourism market and increased educational and community links provide practical examples of the benefits already flowing from this approach. In all of this, no one's political allegiances or aspirations are threatened.

So then, how can change for the better be sustained so that the grosser problems that produce intercommunal tension and confrontation are eliminated? The short answer is political leadership committed to working the partnership institutions of the Good Friday Agreement and that demonstrates support for the reformed and transformed police service and for a human-rights-based approach to resolving disputes over parades and other contentious matters. Such a partnership approach requires that each community accepts the bona fides of the other's cultural identity, political aspirations and allegiances in the terms prescribed by the agreement. If people who describe themselves as republicans cannot respect the Orange tradition as legitimate and that it has a right to the lawful, public expression of its customs, then they are less than republican. If the Orange and other loyal organisations and unionist politicians cannot enter into dialogue and then into working partnerships with nationalists, or cannot respect nationalist traditions and, especially, the religious allegiance of most nationalists, they betray the civil and religious liberties that they claim to defend. Failure to rise to these challenges will have its most serious consequences in the area of community relations. Failure will mean that at best a benign form of apartheid will exist throughout Northern Ireland. At worst the suspicions and hatreds underlying that apartheid will fester and smoulder, risking future explosions of a greater or lesser sort. If Northern Ireland fails to pursue the changes to intercommunal relationships essential to the full implementation of the Good Friday Agreement, its people will have lost the best opportunity to make their society the beacon of hope that the world had expected on that Good Friday morning of 1998. Above all, if the partnership approach cannot be entered into wholeheartedly at all levels of government, local as well as regional, then Northern Ireland will condemn its people to another generation in which age-old tensions will fester and, from time to time, overflow into violent confrontation. Hopefully, with the new dawn promised by the St Andrews' Agreement and the consequent re-establishment of political institutions, such fears will not be realised. Instead, as Una and her father would have wished, the 'elimination of old hatreds, old furies, and the quenching of old fires' between the children of the Planter and the Gael will truly be underway.

Wounds

Michael Longley

Here are two pictures from my father's head –
I have kept them like secrets until now:
First, the Ulster Division at the Somme
Going over the top with 'Fuck the Pope!'
'No Surrender!': a boy about to die,
Screaming 'Give 'em one for the Shankill!'
'Wilder than Gurkhas' were my father's words
Of admiration and bewilderment.
Next comes the London-Scottish padre
Resettling kilts with his swagger-stick,
With a stylish backhand and a prayer.
Over a landscape of dead buttocks
My father followed him for fifty years.
At last, a belated casualty,
He said – lead traces flaring till they hurt –
'I am dying for King and Country, slowly.'
I touched his hand, his thin head I touched.

Now, with military honours of a kind,
With his badges, his medals like rainbows,
His spinning compass, I bury beside him
Three teenage soldiers, bellies full of
Bullets and Irish beer, their flies undone.
A packet of Woodbines I throw in,

A lucifer, the Sacred Heart of Jesus
Paralysed as heavy guns put out
The night-light in a nursery for ever;
Also a bus-conductor's uniform –
He collapsed beside his carpet-slippers
Without a murmur, shot through the head
By a shivering boy who wandered in
Before they could turn the television down
Or tidy away the supper dishes.
To the children, to a bewildered wife,
I think 'Sorry Missus' was what he said.

PART II
RESTRUCTURING

Understanding War

Some Personal Reflections on the Role of the Arts in the Teaching of Ethics

Linda Hogan

On November 19, at eleven o'clock in the morning, as Vukovar's crisis headquarters tried, unsuccessfully, to make contact with the outside world, the JNA [Yugoslav People's Army] entered the hospital complex, the last bastion of Croat resistance. To the terror of those inside they arrived ahead of the international monitors who were to supervise the evacuation. The ICRC truck, carrying medicine for the sick, arrived at six in the evening. By then the JNA had begun to evacuate the sick-and-wounded, without international supervision, and in contravention of the previous day's agreement ... The JNA began to separate the men from the women and children. The latter were asked to choose whether they wanted to be evacuated to Serbia or Croatia [and allowed to leave or handed over to the Croatian authorities] ... The men were not handed over; and many of them – more than three years later, at the time of writing – are presumed dead, buried in a mass grave at Ovčara, outside Vukovar.[1]

Before we take our places in Trial Chamber II at the International Criminal Tribunal for the Former Yugoslavia in The Hague, we read over the indictment against the individuals whose case we are about to observe. It makes for chilling reading.

The accused, Mile Mrkšiç, Miroslav Radiç and Veselin Šljivančanin,[2] are charged on the basis of individual criminal responsibility[3] and superior criminal responsibility[4] with five counts of crimes against humanity[5] and three counts of violations of the laws or customs of war.[6] The indictment alleges that the three individuals before us engaged in the persecution of Croats or other non-Serbs who were present in the Vukovar Hospital through the commission of murder, torture, cruel treatment, extermination and inhumane acts. It further alleges that Miroslav Radiç and Veselin Šljivančanin personally participated in the selection of detainees who were to be loaded on buses. The buses left the hospital and proceeded to the JNA barracks whence some of the detainees were then transported to a farm building in Ovčara, where soldiers beat them. Soldiers then transported their non-Serb captives in groups of about ten to twenty to a ravine in the direction of Grabovo where they killed at least 264 Croats and other non-Serbs from Vukovar Hospital. After the killings the bodies of the victims were buried by bulldozer in a mass grave at the same location.[7]

As we listen to the testimony – on this particular day, it is the then mayor of Vukovar justifying his decision to allow the 'evacuation' prior to the arrival of the international monitors – we struggle to comprehend how the three men before us have come to be charged with such heinous crimes. The historical and political texts we have consulted in advance of our trip help to explain the context. Tim Judah describes how different historical narratives impact on the current political situation[8] and Slavenka Drakulic,[9] though she expresses her incomprehension at the speed and ferocity of the killing, illuminates for us the political culture that helps explain the collective passivity in the face of rising threats. Psychological studies too form part of our picture as we contemplate what it might mean to have committed these crimes. And yet, notwithstanding the cumulative weight of this analysis, our questions persist. Moreover, as the human faces of this atrocity appear before us our conversation turns to whether one can ever really understand the nature of violence and, more particularly, whether the difficulties of understanding and communication are properly appreciated among those who discuss the ethics of war. As we honour the memory of Una

O'Higgins O'Malley, who was deeply committed to the belief that education can and ought to be a vehicle for reconciliation, it seems appropriate to contemplate some of these questions, especially as they arise in the context of teaching.

Problematising the Nature of Violence

There is little doubt that many of the most urgent and intractable issues in politics today revolve around the use of violence for political ends and as a result they inevitably loom large in the classroom as well. Amongst a host of related topics perhaps the most challenging issue for teacher and student alike involves attempting to gain some insight into the nature of violence itself. Indeed it has been this above all else that is most elusive as we listen to the evidence in the trial chamber in The Hague. It is undoubtedly difficult for those of us who have never endured physical violence to understand the havoc that violence creates. Yet those of us who are concerned about the ethical questions raised by war do need to gain some proximity to the perspectives of those who have experienced violence. It is surprising, therefore, that most academic discussions of the ethics of war, whether they be philosophical or theological, seem to by-pass the question of whether the nature of violence can be understood and seem to assume that its nature can be appropriately represented and communicated. In fact, ethical analyses of war rarely keep in view the individual acts of violence that, cumulatively, become the object of in bello assessments of proportionality. And while these texts are adept at debating the merits of the principle of double effect in determining the moral limits of collateral damage, they frequently fail to attend to the particularity of the brutality that stands at the heart of any war. However, it is important that ethical evaluations of war are clear-sighted about the nature of the activity through which war is defined. Moreover, it is essential that they be able to communicate as fully as possible the multiple meanings that the violence of war carries. Indeed, ultimately, if an ethical analysis is to be an honest one then it must begin and end with questions about the moral significance of the particular, with the behaviour of individual men and women, of those who enact and those who experience the horror and brutality of war.

Perhaps it is because violence is so pervasively and persistently represented, and because we effectively live in a 'society of spectacle',[10] that we assume we know what we are talking about when we come to assess the violence that is the essence of war. Yet ethical assessments of war rarely pause to ask what violence requires of the person; what being a perpetrator of acts of violence does to the person; how violence impacts on the victim; to what extent the nature of violence can be communicated; how legitimisations of violence function; and how the hazards of idolatry and self-legitimisation in the creation of justifications for war can be mitigated.[11] Moreover, even when these questions get an airing, the focus of the enquiry tends to be a rather narrow and truncated one that is primarily concerned with its intellectual aspects. In fact, we need to adopt many modes of engagement if we are to appreciate even some of the fundamentals of these questions, with political, historical, philosophical and theological analyses all taking their places. Over the years, however, I have come to believe that, irrespective of the sophistication of our analysis, reason alone will not deliver an understanding of the nature of violence and its impact on victim and victimiser alike. Indeed, it is precisely here that we confront the limits of reason. Rather our questioning needs to leave room for – indeed needs to enable, encourage and even prompt – us to cast ourselves (however imperfectly) in the place of the other, in the hope that we can begin to comprehend the nature of the ethical questions that recourse to violence raises.

Yet how can one imaginatively inhabit the world of one who has lived through a genocide and seen family and friends tortured and killed? Can one ever begin to understand the mind of someone who has committed atrocious acts, who has rounded up the non-Serb male patients in a hospital, led them onto buses and arranged for the disposal of their bodies after they had been murdered? In these contexts there are only partial, faltering answers to such questions. In my teaching I have found that the visual and literary arts are invaluable in the attempt to capture the texture of the ethical questions that are at stake. Indeed, I have concluded that it is the works of the photographers and the poets, even more than the historians or the political theorists, that best illuminate the ethical sensibilities in question. There are a host of scholarly analyses that discuss the relationship between the aesthetic and the ethical and that enable one to reflect on the more theoretical aspects of the issue at hand. Moreover, in recent years ethicists have increasingly attended to autobiography, testimonial literature and other literary sources in the attempt to better understand the ethical questions that war raises.[12] A fuller discussion of the role of the arts in considering the ethics of war would necessarily need to attend to these concerns. My purpose in this context, however, is a more modest one: it is to discuss some of the pieces of art that I have used in my own teaching on the ethics of war, with the intention of reflecting on what and how they teach about the nature of violence. My focus here is on some visual pieces, in part because they are so rarely reflected on by ethicists, but more importantly because I have found that they create a context in which the emotional, intellectual and spiritual aspects of the enactment of violence not only can, but also must, be addressed.

Representing the Unrepresentable

> These dead are supremely uninterested in the living: in those who took their lives; in witnesses – and in us. Why should they seek our gaze? What would they have to say to us? 'We' – this 'we' is everyone who has never experienced anything like they went through – don't understand. We don't get it. We truly can't imagine what it was like. We can't imagine how dreadful, how terrifying war is; and how normal it becomes. Can't understand, can't imagine. That's what every soldier, and every journalist and aid worker and independent observer who has put in time under fire, and had the luck to elude the death that struck down others nearby, stubbornly feels. And they are right.[13]

In a world where visual representations of violence abound, and in which the sheer volume of these images can lead to the desensitisation of our critical and emotional capacities, it is easy to dismiss the moral power of such representations. Moreover, Susan Sontag is correct to insist that the viewer ought to be aware of the limits of what can be expressed and communicated with respect to the enactment of violence. And yet, as she recognises in *Regarding the Pain of Others,* particular photographs and video installations can indeed capture those aspects of violence that are not amenable to easy representation and, as a result, can create a context in which the moral questions can be raised in a different register. Moreover, this is the case regardless of how graphic or otherwise the representation may be. Of course, constantly in one's mind are questions about how the line between voyeurism and glamorisation on the one hand and truthful communication on the other can be drawn. Yet despite the ambivalence of many visual images, they often prompt us to ask questions that rarely surface in discussions about the ethics of war, most especially when they force us to think about the enactment of violence in its totality and in the context of the impact it has on victim and survivors and on victimisers.

Most ethical appraisals of war are silent about the impact of violence and have only rarely recognised the difficulties involved in apprehending what the enactment of violence does to, and requires of, the person. WarningSHOTS!, an exhibition of contemporary art that explored conflict and violence, which toured a number of cities in Great Britain in 2000, included a number of visual pieces that, without resorting to melodrama or sentimentality, conveyed an understanding of some aspects of the nature of violence that are unusually difficult to represent. The pieces by Monica Oechsler, Willie Doherty and Christine Borland were especially striking in terms of challenging the viewer to connect with particular aspects of violence. With her four-and-a-half-minute video entitled Strip, played in continuous loop, Monica Oechsler creates in the viewer an escalating sense of foreboding and terror as young girls strip down and reassemble handguns, singing nursery rhymes as they do so. The girls were from the only British gun-club licensed to have members as young as eight years old. We only see the girls from the neck down as they expertly strip their guns and put them back together again. Our foreboding rises because, having initially been soothed and somewhat mesmerised by their rhythmic singing of nursery rhymes, it gradually begins to dawn on us that they do not understand the power they have with the loaded weapons in their hands. We wonder what they intend to do; who they are; whether they can be trusted not to shoot; whether they are damaged or traumatised in some way. Of course, their youth and the juxtaposition of the nursery rhymes with lethal weapons accentuates the sense of foreboding, yet it is the fluency with which they handle these weapons, the fascination that their power holds and, most of all, the sheer arbitrariness of the 'decision' to use the guns that creates the sense of menace. In another exhibit, Willie Doherty's photograph At the Border V (Isolated Incident) presents us with an image of a stained and torn mattress dumped by the roadside somewhere in Northern Ireland. Of course, the context imbues this not uncommon sight of a discarded mattress with a particular significance, since we know that the holes in the mattress are most likely bullet holes. In this image the pitiless isolation of both victim and victimiser is vividly and unbearably on show. The viewer is immediately prompted to ask what it would mean to have this as one's last encounter in life, one's final experience and memory. Moreover, one is forced to ask what it would mean to be the one who walked away from this scene having inflicted lethal violence on another person, who was most likely a neighbour, a colleague or even a friend. The shocking finality and absurdity of violence is expertly evoked in Christine Borland's installation The Quickening, the Lightening, the Crowning. The viewer enters a dark walled space (a womb?) in which is displayed anatomical models of childbirth while one listens to a soundtrack of a foetal heartbeat running continuously. Overlayed is another soundtrack, this time of gunfire created with the guns that were handed over to the police during the amnesty that followed the Dunblane killings.[14] The juxtaposition of the protective space and the strong, rhythmic foetal heartbeat with the roar of the gun expresses better than the most subtle of arguments the beauty and preciousness of the single life and brings us face to face with the radical destructiveness that such weapons bring.

Sontag may well be correct that those of us who have not experienced war 'can't imagine how dreadful, how terrifying war is; and how normal it becomes. Can't understand, can't imagine'. Yet Oechsler, Doherty and Borland, in their respective ways, hold our gaze and require us to look again at the practice that is war. The arts, visual and literary, enable the viewer to raise the ethical questions in a different way. They help us to think about what it means to participate in acts of brutality; they prompt us to think about the lure of violence, about the nature of accountability, about the vulnerabilities of ordinary people, about complicity and about the abdication of responsibility. Most of all, perhaps, they issue a summons, a summons to abandon the fictional realities about war that we have created and, ultimately, a summons to acknowledge, head-on, the horror that is war. In her magisterial *Foundations of Violence*, the late Grace Jantzen argues that we will only be able to resist what she calls the 'necrophilic habitus of modernity' once we have begun to construct alternative political, ethical and religious discourses – that is, discourses that no longer sacralise or justify violence.[15] There is no doubt that the arts can make a distinctive and unique contribution to the construction of alternative discourses, not least in what they teach us about the nature of violence.

> Much of what is narrowly termed politics seems to rest on a longing for certainty even at the cost of honesty; for an analysis that, once given, need not be re-examined … Truthfulness everywhere means heightened complexity … The politics worth having, the relationships worth having, demand that we delve still deeper.[16]

Notes

1   Laura Silber and Allan Little, *The Death of Yugoslavia*, Harmondsworth, Penguin Books, 1996, pp. 179–80.

2   According to the indictment, the accused held the following positions during the relevant period:
Mile Mrkšiç was a colonel in the JNA and commander of the 1st Guards Motorised Brigade and Operational Group South. After the fall of Vukovar, he was promoted to general rank in the JNA and became the commander of the 8th JNA Operational Group in the Kordun area in Croatia. Following the withdrawal of the JNA from Croatia in 1992, he returned to the Federal Republic of Yugoslavia and occupied several posts in the VJ General Staff. He became the commanding officer of the army of the so-called 'Republic of Serb

Krajina' (RSK) in May 1995.

Miroslav Radiç was a captain in the JNA. He commanded an infantry company in the 1st Battalion of the 1st Guards Motorised Brigade.

Veselin Šljivančanin was a major in the JNA. He was the security officer of the 1st Guards Motorised Brigade and Operational Group South and as such was de facto in charge of a military police battalion subordinated to the 1st Guards Motorised Brigade. After the fall of Vukovar, Šljivančanin was promoted to the rank of lieutenant colonel and was placed in command of the VJ brigade in Podgorica, Montenegro.

3   Article 7(1) of the Statute.

4   Article 7(3) of the Statute.

5   Article 5 of the Statute – persecutions on political, racial and religious grounds; extermination; murder; torture; inhumane acts.

6   Article 3 of the Statute – murder; torture; cruel treatment.

7   Mrkšiç et al., case IT-95-13/1, www.un.org/icty.

8   Tim Judah, *The Serbs: History, Myth and the Destruction of Yugoslavia*, New Haven, Yale University Press, 1997.

9   *They Would Never Hurt a Fly: War Criminals on Trial*, London, Abacus Books, 2004.

10   Susan Sontag, *Regarding the Pain of Others*, New York, Farrar, Straus and Giroux, 2002, p. 109.

11   See Gerhard Beestermöller, 'Eurocentricity in the Perception of Wars', *Concilium* (2001/2), pp. 33–42; Irina Novikova, 'Lessons from the Anatomy of War: Svetlana Alexievich's Zinky Boys', pp. 99–116 and Rada Drezgiç, 'Demographic Nationalism in the Gender Perspective', pp. 211–35, in Svetlana Slapšak, *War Discourse, Women's Discourse Essays and Case-studies from Yugoslavia and Russia*, Ljubljana, TOPOS, 2000.

12   See, for example, Sumner Twiss, 'Humanities and Atrocities: Some Reflections', *Journal of the Society of Christian Ethics*, Vol. 25, No. 1 (2005), pp. 219–34 and the response by Paul Lauritzen, pp. 235–48.

13   Sontag, op. cit., p. 126, commenting on Jeff Wall's 1992 image entitled Dead Troops Talk (A Vision after an Ambush of a Red Army Patrol near Moqor, Afghanistan, Winter 1986).

14   In 1996 a Mr Hamilton entered a primary school in Dunblane, Scotland, and killed sixteen children and a schoolteacher. In the aftermath the police declared an amnesty for those who held illegal handguns.

15   Grace Jantzen, *Foundations of Violence*, London, Routledge, 2004, p. 10.

16   Adrienne Rich, *The Arts of the Possible*, New York, W.W. Norton, 2001, p. 39.

Blessed Are The Peacemakers

Dennis Kennedy

BLESSED ARE THE PEACEMAKERS ... for theirs is a growth industry and who today dares question their motives, their integrity and their wisdom? Their ranks include pop stars and presidents, priests and prelates, magnates and models, actors and academics. They have been unstinting in their efforts, from Belfast to Beirut, from Colombo to Columbia, from the Middle East to East Timor, from Sudan to Cyprus. They win prizes and plaudits, they make headlines and sometimes, but not very often, they make peace. They also make, if not enemies, then critics and opponents who are unimpressed by their good intentions and wish they would stay at home. Such cynicism is understandable as regards the travels of Mr Adams and Mr McGuinness to the Basque country, Palestine or Sri Lanka to share their expertise. But it is much more widespread.

In fairness, celebrity peacemakers have been applauded and rewarded not for making peace but for trying. They are not paid by results. Away from the headlines there are hosts of others, many of whom volunteer their time and energy in the search for peace, who work, as individuals or members of groups, for reconciliation, understanding, rapprochement and reunion. Others write theses and learned tomes on peacemaking and heroically attend endless rounds of peace conferences and seminars. Yet these too have their critics. All the while the world becomes less, not more, peaceful and if we were less afraid of appearing heartless reactionaries, many more of us would own up to feelings of cynicism extending to antipathy and distaste for peace movements and peacemakers.

Why should this be? Confronted with political violence inflicting immeasurable suffering on our fellow human beings, surely the only civilised response is to cry out for peace and applaud the efforts of all who work for it? No doubt there is resentment of well-intentioned outsiders who meddle in our affairs, impatience with those who know far less about the problem than we do and frustration with those who proffer simple solutions to what we know are complex challenges. There is too, almost certainly, a mixture of guilt and fatigue felt by those among us who have wrestled with the insoluble for years when confronted with the naive optimism of the enthusiastic peacemaker. But there is also an uneasiness that even the best-intentioned peacemaking can confuse the picture and can be exploited by those whose priority is political advantage rather than peace. In today's world there are two basic elements to most conflicts. One is a fundamental political problem bringing groups of people into dispute with each other – over territory, language, identity, religion. The second element is the use of violence in such a situation to secure a political end.

Since Cain and Abel, mankind has used violence to settle arguments: tribes fought each other, then feudal lords, then kings and emperors, then alliances and axes. It was only after 1945 that we began to see, particularly in Europe and the US, a generalised rejection of violence as a legitimate means of achieving political objectives. A characteristic of many of today's 'problems' is the rejection of that consensus and the use of violence to fast-forward, reverse, thwart or distort the resolution of differences by non-violent means such as discussion, negotiation and democratic decision making. The terms 'terrorism' and 'terrorist', though regarded as unhelpful by some in the peace industry, are valid in that they convey the reality of politically motivated violence in western society. Violence is used, not to defeat an organised enemy by force of arms, but to subvert the democratic process by bullying populations and, more easily, governments into accepting demands hitherto found unacceptable. Its methods are murder, sometimes mass murder, and destruction, and the designation 'terrorist' conveys an appropriate sense of the worst type of criminality. Western democratic governments have wrestled unsuccessfully with political terrorism for decades. Meeting violence with force, special powers of arrest and detention and measures to restrict the activities of terrorist-linked organisations may, for a time, be effective but generally risk alienating sections of the population and possibly enlarging sympathy and support for the terrorist groups. Use of the police to enforce such measures can make policing difficult, if not impossible, among people affected. As the experience in Northern Ireland has shown, the army, any army, is not designed for a civil role and its use can cause more problems than it solves. Into this dangerous quagmire come the peacemakers, motivated by a genuine desire to stop the violence and the suffering it inflicts, convinced that dialogue and political accommodation offer the only real path to peace. Peacemakers may come in from outside, often by invitation, or they may already be in situ, like the Peace People of the 1970s or the various cross-community groups that have arisen. Governments, like those in London and Dublin, despairing of winning a war against terrorism may genuinely see a 'peace initiative' as a means of solving the problem.

Not everyone boarding the peace bandwagon has such honourable motivation: it may be a convenient tactic for those more concerned with immediate advantage than long-term peace. Terrorists, realising they cannot win by physical force, may hope to win political concessions and save face in the short term. Governments, too, weary of fighting terrorism may see it as a way to wash their hands of the problem with a modicum of dignity. But the dubious motives of some on board should not be cited to discredit the entire enterprise. There are more fundamental concerns that arise from methods of working which are characteristic of most peace processes.

- Almost all peace initiatives call for dialogue, and that dialogue, sooner or later, includes those who have been engaged in promoting or perpetrating violence.
- A basis for dialogue is the assumption that both sides have some validity as regards their underlying demands.
- History will be extensively rewritten to accommodate this assumption.
- Peace processes tend to develop a language of their own that makes criticism difficult and hampers intelligent discussion.

If these characteristics are examined in the context of the peace process that has evolved in Northern Ireland over the past decade or two, some of the pitfalls can be illustrated. Dialogue is the obvious alternative to armed conflict but democratic governments, including those in London and Dublin, for years affirmed, as a matter of principle, that they would never talk to terrorists, would never negotiate with people seeking to subvert the democratic process by force of arms. Those two governments still subscribe to that doctrine through their adherence to the European Union's refusal to deal with Hamas in Palestine. London, supported by Dublin, was still loudly affirming this stance as regards the IRA even after it had started secret talks with that organisation. It can be argued that the IRA ceasefires and the undeniable reduction in violence could not have been achieved otherwise – only by engaging the men of violence and reaching some sort of accommodation with them could their reason, or excuse, for violence be removed.

But there lies the fault: in a democracy there never was, and never can be, any excuse for resorting to violence for political ends. The moment a democratic government enters into dialogue with a group that has not renounced violence and that retains arms, it concedes some degree of legitimacy to the use of violence. A graphic demonstration of this can be seen in the remarkable rise in electoral support for Sinn Féin in Northern Ireland, running alongside public welcome for and acceptance of republican leaders in London and Dublin. In practice, the dialogue inevitably centres on the demands of the violent group, even though it may, initially, have little public backing. An enormous sacrifice of principle has been made. The question remains whether it has really eliminated violence and resolved the fundamental political issue. Could it, in fact, have gone some way towards sanitising, if not sanctifying, violence and making the underlying political problem even more intractable?

An ever-present element in any peace process is even-handedness, the assumption that every side has a legitimate point of view and demand. An almost universal mantra of peace movements is that there are 'faults on both sides' or 'we are all guilty'. While both are doubtless true, they are also invitations, on the one hand to regard one's own guilt or fault as somehow cancelled out by those of the other side, and on the other to ignore the underlying political dispute. This can mean that in the dash for peace there is no serious examination of the fundamental issue. Instead all energy is devoted to finding a way to accommodate the demands of those engaging in violence. Here the basic nationalist demand for the incorporation of Northern Ireland into an independent Irish state is treated in the Belfast Agreement as perfectly reasonable, something that will be facilitated as soon as there is a majority for it in the province. But such territorial nationalism has no validity in today's Europe and is a hangover from the nineteenth century, as is the very concept of national identity that permeates the agreement. The formula in the agreement, that all can change as soon as a bare majority wishes, is never examined in relation to its impact on the stability of the current situation, nor in the context of what might actually happen if 50 per cent plus one did actually vote for change. Instead every phrase is tuned to give maximum assurance to nationalism that its currently impossible demand will one day be granted.

It is to avoid the awkward historical reality that an irreconcilable population in one part of the island made partition the inevitable price of independence for the rest that there has been a rush to rewrite history, and in particular to accept the version of history invented by Sinn Féin. Thus we repeatedly hear that the IRA campaign was a struggle for justice and equality, that the position of the nationalist minority in Northern Ireland was such that resort to armed revolt was understandable, if not inevitable. This is a myth. There is ample evidence to prove that it is a fabrication, though here it may be sufficient to cite John Hume's repeated assertion that, for the whole period, there was no issue in Northern Ireland worth the taking of a single life. The myth has, however, served to obscure the nature of the underlying problem. Great efforts have been made, through legislation and institutions, to ensure the fairest possible society in Northern Ireland as a means to peace. But the IRA has not been fighting for a better Northern Ireland: it has been using terror as a means of pursuing Irish nationalism's territorial claim to the whole island.

The German philologist Victor Klemperer, whose diaries of life as a Jew in Dresden under Nazi rule must rank as the most important diaries of the twentieth century, also wrote a book called *The Language of the Third Reich,* analysing how the regime's deliberate manipulation of language was used to condition the German people to Nazi thinking and actions. In Northern Ireland a whole lexicon has been developed. What has, essentially, been a negotiated settlement with an armed terrorist organisation is invariably termed a 'peace process'. Who can oppose such a process without seeming to oppose peace itself? The Belfast Agreement, as it was originally named and is referred to in legislation, rapidly became the Good Friday Agreement, not just because it was concluded on that day, but also because someone decided there was PR value in the name. That same agreement, which was hailed as ending the longest terrorist campaign in twentieth-century Europe, never once mentions the words 'terrorist' or 'terrorism'. The expression used is 'paramilitary organisation' – acceptable to all assorted terrorist bands in Ireland. When the question of illegally held weapons arose, the governments, and all those engaged in the misnamed peace process, scrupulously eschewed any suggestion that terrorists should surrender their weapons in accordance with the law. Instead the deceitful term 'decommissioning' was adopted. The act of commissioning suggests a legitimate exercise of authority, an official sanction; decommissioning weapons, therefore, is something that only a legally constituted and recognised army could do. So asking the IRA to decommission its weapons, at time, place and method of its own choosing, implies that those weapons were held, in some unspecified way, legitimately.

All this is extremely dangerous ground in the context of the history of Irish nationalism since the early twentieth century. Violence as a part of that tradition goes back at least to 1798 and the United Irishmen, but since 1916 it has been revered by many as a higher manifestation of nationalism, as the most elevated expression of the right to national freedom, and Irish unity. In 1922 the new Irish state had, indeed, to defend itself vigorously against subversive violence waged against it in the name of Irish nationalism and has thereafter set its face officially against it.

But the tradition has survived and has had substantial support, overt and covert, in mainline political parties in the South at various periods since.

Among the most dramatic outcomes of the peace process in Northern Ireland is massive backing in the nationalist community for Sinn Féin, the party inextricably linked to the IRA and the vociferous defenders of the right of Irish republicans to use violence for political ends. While the violence has largely stopped, and Sinn Féin no longer justifies its use, the tradition remains intact and the terrorists of the past three decades are gaining daily in their status as heroes and martyrs. The celebrations in 2006 to mark the sixtieth anniversary of the Easter Rising showed again the ambivalence towards political violence that lies close to the heart of Irish nationalism. This island still desperately needs peacemakers but they should identify their objectives much more carefully and clearly. Their prime target must be to eradicate the cult of violence as a legitimate feature of Irish nationalism. The worst possible way to set about this is to grant concession after concession to the apostles of violence in the hope that they will no longer feel any need to use it or have any excuse for doing so. Their second target should be the bad history that increasingly obscures the fundamental issue and prevents the serious questioning of the myths and fabrications that still persuade the voters to vote as they do. There is a wealth of good scholarship but it is not reflected in debate on the problem, neither in government and political circles in London and Dublin nor in most of the media.

The title for this collection of essays is *Remembering to Forgive*. Many current attempts at peacemaking seem founded on the contrary premise that to forgive one must also forget. Collective amnesia might make peacemaking a lot easier but it is not on offer.

Future of Northern Ireland

Garret FitzGerald

PARTITION, IMPOSED IN 1920, eventually proved to have a powerful dynamic of its own as both parts of the island of Ireland began to pursue their own very different goals. It was, of course, a British government that for its own reasons effected the geographical partitioning of Ireland into two polities. But thereafter it was successive governments of the new Irish state, in the first of which Una O'Higgins O'Malley's father and mine were ministers, which progressively deepened that division by seeking to effect a radical change in the ethos of the area under their jurisdiction. They did this primarily through an Irish-language revival programme, using the schools and the public service, and also later by giving the new state's laws and constitution a Catholic tinge – although both W.T. Cosgrave and Eamon de Valera rejected the concept of a 'Catholic State' such as the Vatican wished to see in Ireland. Neither of these ministers was personally 'fanatic about Gaelic', as Kevin O'Higgins once explained to Leo Amery, Dominions Secretary. My father, although personally attached to the language, had accepted in May 1919 that English was the language of Ireland even more than French was the language of France.

In this process everyone grossly underestimated the extent to which a loyalty to the new Irish state on the part of its inhabitants would quickly replace any real, as distinct from sentimental, sense of an all-island Irishness. By contrast, the North changed much less – although, of course, Protestant fears and reactions in that area perpetuated Catholic alienation. Paradoxically, whilst Southerners were losing their sense of an all-Ireland Irishness as a result of their new loyalty to their own state, Northern

Protestants never lost a sense of being a threatened minority in the island as a whole rather than a secure majority in their own polity. Both peoples were eventually left with a sense of guilt about the way they reacted to their new situation. In the South for decades this sense of guilt was easily assuaged by rhetorical anglo-phobic, anti-partition irredentism – which was given free rein until the outbreak of violence in the North forced a fundamental rethink of that stance by the political class between 1969 and 1972. That rethink soon led to a belated recognition (public on the part of Fine Gael and Labour but private for several decades thereafter on the part of Fianna Fáil) that the interests of the Irish state actually lay in seeking jointly with Britain to create a stable and peaceful Northern Ireland that would remain within the UK until such time as a majority in the North might, perhaps, decide otherwise. And, at the same time, recognition was growing that there was also a need to rethink the neo-Gaelic Catholic uniculturalism that had marked the new Irish state from its foundation.

Twenty years were, however, to elapse, between the early 1970s and the early 1990s, before all political parties in the Irish state felt able publicly and unambiguously to adopt both the concept of pluralism as the ethos of their state and the principle of consent as a necessary basis for Irish unity – and before a British government for its part recognised the futility of seeking an end to the violence by unfocused and consequently counter-productive security, instead of facing up to the positive political steps that needed to be taken to win back fading support for constitutional nationalism, in a way that would eventually force the IRA to abandon its armalite and ballot box policy in favour of one based only on the ballot box. The final acceptance by all but a tiny minority of irreconcilable republicans North and South of the consent principle has now created the conditions for the belated emergence of a stable Northern Ireland polity that may in time be accepted and endorsed by all its people.

The reality is that, to an even greater extent than in the cases of Scotland and Wales, Northern Ireland has domestic needs different from those of much larger England: different in respect of such issues as strategic investment, industrial development, agriculture, regional policy and education – but also in having to carry through a painful transition from a security-dominated to a normal society. To someone from the South, the revived form of devolved government of Northern Ireland briefly and temporarily established some time after the Belfast Agreement seemed to work quite well at what may be called the 'operational level'. The successful preparation by that body of a draft programme for the future, the constructive ways in which all ministers tackled their individual tasks and the positive spirit in which the new North–South relationship began – all these were encouraging, although the subsequent, prolonged hiatus has, perhaps, obscured these positive aspects of the new devolved system of government.

That a relatively constructive approach marked the early work of this new devolved administration – despite the fact that one party in it was still linked to a paramilitary body and that another felt unable to join with its partners at executive meetings – suggests that, with the resolution of the political crisis, a reformed executive, responsible to the assembly, may eventually prove a dynamic force for the future development of Northern Ireland. Because this involves the development of new and contemporary structures not burdened by a historic heritage of customs and precedents – as unhappily are the governments of both Britain and the Republic – a devolved executive in Northern Ireland seems to me to have a huge potential capacity for innovative action, based on a very close relationship with the people of the area it governs. As to the North–South relationship: freed from the shadow of Articles 2 and 3 of the Irish Constitution, this, I believe, enjoys great possibilities for constructive action, especially in relation to matters where neither part of the island is big enough on its own to maximise its potential – energy and tourism are good examples. This has already been demonstrated by the early work of the North–South Ministerial Council and the progress made with their briefs by the implementation bodies as they await fresh political inputs.

It is important that residual unionist fears about closer relations with the Republic, which logically should have been removed by the acceptance of the consent principle by the government and people of the Republic, as well as by nationalists and also republicans in Northern Ireland, should not inhibit joint action in the economic sphere in cases where Northern

Ireland would be a net beneficiary. Accordingly, I have to say I regret that among the brief list of areas agreed for North–South action industrial development was not included. This is an activity in respect of which the Republic has a remarkable record of achievement, through the work of the highly sophisticated Industrial Development Authority. It has long seemed to me that a single, all-Ireland IDA, organised on a basis that would ensure equal treatment for both areas, could have a powerful impact on industrial development in Northern Ireland. For in this as in some other important matters, the Republic has the capacity, and I would hope the will, to assist the Northern Ireland economy, helping it to make some progress in catching up on both the South and the United Kingdom in the years ahead – a point to which I shall return. That potential should be fully exploited, as should the possibility of working together in relation to those aspects of the European's Union's impact on Ireland, in respect of which the interests of Northern Ireland may happen to be closer to those of the Republic than to those of Great Britain.

Of course, there remain many problems to be overcome, above all the traumatised state of unionist opinion, which in part reflects that community's lack of strong and positive political leaderships. I want in conclusion to draw attention to three longer-term issues facing a Northern Ireland with its own devolved government.

Sectarian Political Structure
First, as the Alliance Party never tires of pointing out, the political foundations of the new structures are essentially sectarian. The Constitution of Northern Ireland, as it emerged seven years ago, is based on balancing politically two distinct communities. It discourages the emergence of normal political divisions along the lines of divergent views as to how far the initial market-driven distribution of resources arising from the working of a capitalist system needs to be modified by state-organised redistributive action – and that is, of course, the issue that provides the key element for normal politics in most democratic societies. At least in the early stages of the new Northern Ireland such issues are going to have to be fought out and decided within a government structure that is predetermined by quite different forces – ones that cut right across

such a socioeconomic value divide. How will this work? And how, if at all, can this system ever become normalised within a Northern Ireland context? This issue must in time come to preoccupy all those who wish to see Northern Ireland becoming a normal democratic society.

The Sectarian Demographic Factor

The second issue to which I want to draw attention is the potential effect of demographic change in Northern Ireland. It is clear that in justifying the abandonment of violence and future reliance on the democratic process, the Sinn Féin leadership have relied heavily on what they have claimed to be the prospect of an emerging Catholic nationalist majority – an outcome some of them have convinced themselves to be achievable by perhaps as early as 2016. Earlier in this decade this demographic illusion was accompanied by rumours spread in advance of the 2001 Census suggesting that enumeration would reveal that people of a Catholic background already constituted 46–47 per cent of Northern Ireland's population. That particular balloon was punctured by the publication of the 2001 Census results which, when appropriate allowance is made for a very small number who refused to state their religious background or who say they have no religion, indicate that about 44.5 per cent of today's population comes from a Catholic background – as does about 42 per cent of the adult population, namely the electorate.

Projected forwards, these figures suggest that even if the fertility rate of Catholics continued to be higher than, or at the very least equal to, that of Protestants – an assumption upon which recent trends in Catholic countries of southern Europe cast considerable doubt – all other things being equal, some thirty years would be likely to elapse before the electorate could contain a majority of voters from a Catholic background. That time-scale might, however, be somewhat foreshortened if, despite a political settlement and the return of normal conditions to Northern Ireland, the proportion of Protestant young people going to Britain for higher education and staying away thereafter remained – as was the case in the late 1990s – about twice as high as in the case of young people of Catholic background. (The impact of this could be equivalent to a 7.5 per cent difference in the birth rate of the two communities.)

However, the issue of whether Northern Ireland is to remain in the United Kingdom or to unite politically with the Republic is not going to be decided by a simple religious head-count. Throughout most of the 1990s, annual surveys of opinion in Northern Ireland showed that a significant minority of Catholics – usually close to 35 per cent – expressed a consistent preference for remaining in the United Kingdom. Since the Belfast Agreement this view has been expressed by a smaller proportion of Catholics polled – currently, I understand, around 25 per cent. On this basis, there would seem at present to be a current two-to-one majority in favour of Northern Ireland remaining part of the United Kingdom. Thus for a majority in favour of Irish unity to emerge amongst the Northern Ireland electorate it would be necessary for all of three things to happen: for the Catholic fertility rate to remain indefinitely at or above that of Protestants; for Protestant third-level emigration to remain at twice the Catholic level; and finally for the one-quarter of Catholics who have hitherto favoured remaining in the United Kingdom to change their minds on that issue.

The fact that a majority in favour of Irish political unity is thus not likely to emerge within the next quarter of a century, and might not emerge thereafter, does not mean, however, that concern about such a development might not, in the period ahead, remain a destabilising factor amongst elements of the Protestant community, especially as republicans will have an interest in keeping this particular pot boiling. On the other hand, this changing demographic situation should over time also offer a strong incentive to unionists to act in such a way as to encourage elements in the Catholic community to maintain their support for continued participation in the United Kingdom.

Northern Ireland's Over-Dependence on the UK

A third issue affecting Northern Ireland's future is that of its capacity for economic growth. Back in the second half of the 1960s, the economies of both Northern Ireland and the Republic were growing at a rate of over 4 per cent a year – much faster than that of Britain, where the growth rate was then about 2.25 per cent. Writing about Northern Ireland in 1972, in a book entitled *Towards a New Ireland*, I was emboldened to suggest that if that disparity between these growth rates of Ireland, North and South, and of Britain were to persist, both parts of this island could catch up with Britain within a quarter of a century. So far as the Republic is concerned, I was nearly right in that projection, for despite the mess made of its economy at the end of the 1970s, which lost us eight years of growth, Irish GNP per head is now within 5 per cent of the UK level.

Northern Ireland, however, was less fortunate. From the early 1970s onwards its growth rate slowed, partly because of the gradual disappearance of its declining industries and also because of the violence fomented by the IRA. Nevertheless, although Northern Ireland's growth slowed, during those thirty years it succeeded in catching up slightly on Britain, reducing the shortfall vis-à-vis the overall UK level of output per head from 30 per cent to about 25 per cent.

However, most strikingly, because of very much faster growth in the Republic, Northern Ireland's output has since fallen far behind that of the South: when I first compared the two Irish economies in a 1956 study, the North was then responsible for 37–38 per cent of the output of the island of Ireland – it now produces only 23–24 per cent of that output. (If any of you are surprised at such a huge widening of the economic gap between North and South, well, so was I when this ratio emerged from my research a couple of years ago. I checked my figures with the relevant expert in the Northern Ireland administration, who confirmed that my figures sounded about right to him.) UK government regional figures for 2001, the latest figures available, show the per capita output of Northern Ireland in that year to have been 21–22 per cent below the UK level – and as the Republic's per capita output figure is now only about 5 per cent below that of Britain, that puts Northern Ireland's economic performance about 16–17 per cent – one-sixth, in other words – below that of the Republic. If I am right in feeling that Northern Ireland's living standards are still slightly higher than those of the Republic, this means that transfers from Britain must account for at least 20 per cent – and probably somewhat more – of the income of the area.

Another way of measuring the dependence of Northern Ireland on transfers from Britain is by reference to the proportion of output absorbed by private consumption. The European average ratio of private consumption to GDP is 58 per cent. In Britain the proportion of output consumed is somewhat higher but in Northern Ireland it is an astonishing 80 per cent. That means that a very high proportion of its investment and public spending has to be financed by Britain. (Recently the Northern Ireland economy has been showing some resilience. During the post-2000 recession its growth rate was very little lower than that of the Republic but in the past two years it has once again been failing to match the 5 per cent-plus growth rate of the Republic.) Now there is, of course, nothing surprising about an outlying region of a country having a lower level of output than the country as a whole or of inter-regional transfers being needed to compensate for this. Indeed such an economic relationship between regions is quite normal. In the Republic some counties derive 4–6 per cent of their disposable income from net transfers (excess of state social transfers over taxes paid to the state). But, when there is disparity of as much as 20 per cent, this creates the kind of problem that has bedevilled East Germany since its reunification with West Germany in 1990. Such a high degree of dependence on transfers from the rest of the state to which it belongs is hugely debilitating for any region, with the public sector squeezing out private enterprise, and is very difficult to escape from. A region is very limited in the policies it can adopt and implement in order to generate growth, and the metropolitan government tends to be particularly reluctant to allow any region to use tax incentives for this purpose, lest this lead to an undermining of the whole national tax structure through competitive tax cutting by other regions.

The Republic of Ireland has succeeded in virtually catching up with the UK since 1993 in terms of output per head – because, as I pointed out earlier, of an unexpected and unrepeatable combination of circumstances: a uniquely rapid 4.5 per cent annual growth of labour supply (due to one-off demographic factors unique to the Irish state) combined with the attraction of a quite disproportionate share of US high-tech investment in Europe. It did so by deploying, under exceptionally favourable demographic conditions, a range of policies – including a very low rate of corporate taxation – that were open to it as a sovereign state. Some major factors contributing to that exceptional outcome are not currently available to Northern Ireland – most notably the 12.5 per cent corporate tax rate – but also the non-specialised secondary-education system and the supplementation of its university system with a network of regional technical colleges and institutes of technology. These factors have enabled the Republic to achieve an overall domestic third-level entry rate rapidly approaching 60 per cent and its rate of emigration for undergraduate third-level education is only about one-fifth that of Northern Ireland: the Republic does not suffer from the kind of third-level brain drain that is such a disturbing and debilitating feature of Northern Ireland society.

Devolution will offer Northern Ireland the possibility of addressing some, but not all, of these problems. Whilst it may be difficult for it to catch up with the rest of the UK in terms of output per head, as the Republic has virtually done, there is certainly room for some narrowing of that gap. What has already been achieved in Northern Ireland in difficult circumstances has been quite impressive, for example the increase of one-quarter in the numbers at work in Northern Ireland since 1986 – almost twice the British increase for that period. And although the current low level of unemployment in the North means that an available labour supply no longer offers a significant source of additional workers, the number of eighteen-year-olds in the Northern Irish population is one-sixth higher than in the rest of Europe and a final peace settlement should release workers from the security sector. Even more striking has been the huge increase in manufacturing productivity in Northern Ireland between 1996 and 2001 – although, as in the Republic, this naturally came to an end in face of the recent slowing-down of global economic growth.

A peaceful and stable Northern Ireland, enjoying widespread external goodwill, with its own devolved government in which representatives of both communities work together harmoniously would have an opportunity to reduce substantially its debilitating over-dependence on very large-scale transfers from Britain and perhaps to recover some of the self-reliance and economic dynamism of earlier times. For its economy is no longer being pulled down by the decline of its older industries – shipbuilding and traditional engineering, textiles and clothing: that process has effectively been completed. But for Northern Ireland's economy to catch up with that of Great Britain to a sufficient degree to reduce transfers to a tolerable level will be very difficult indeed. And it is not generally realised that this economic factor poses an even greater long-term obstacle to political unification of the island than the British allegiance of unionists, with their commitment to remaining part of the United Kingdom. For even if the factor of unionist Britishness were to diminish substantially, the cost in terms of loss of transfers from Britain and the potential impact of political unification on Northern living standards could generate economic rather than political opposition to such unity – amongst Catholics as well as amongst Protestants. And one would need to be a remarkable optimist to believe that the electorate in the Republic would be willing to replace lost transfers from Britain, which, because of the population disparity between these two sovereign states, would weigh fifteen times more heavily on the taxpayers of the Irish state than they now do on the – largely unaware – taxpayers of Britain.

For my own part, I regret that this is where we in this island now find ourselves. I have always believed that it would have been much better – socially and economically – for all our people in this island to have joined together in a sovereign state eighty-five years ago rather than to have been divided between two states whose people and governments, perhaps inevitably, both foolishly set about creating in each of the jurisdictions two divergent, backward-looking, unicultural enclaves. In that sense I am an Irish nationalist – but a pluralist nationalist. However, the fact that this is what both sentiment and reason have led me to feel does not mean that I can blind myself to the realities of the Ireland in which we find ourselves at the start of the twenty-first century. I should be delighted if someone could show me a credible economic path towards an all-Ireland state – if the political obstacles were by some miracle to disappear. Unhappily, I have yet to hear anyone even address this issue – never mind attempting to show how it might be resolved. There is room for quite radical change in border areas if in the new situation the damage done to these areas by partition can be undone. But this will not be easy. Vested interests have grown up on either side of the border that will not easily be dislodged.

Smuggling is one of these – and some Sinn Féin/IRA members have a strong interest in keeping this going. Moreover, the factors that create an opportunity for money to be made from smuggling do not fall within the combined competence of the political authorities North and South. Taxes imposed on hydrocarbons in Northern Ireland are decided by the Westminster government, and whilst in theory it would be open to the Irish government to wipe out smuggling of hydrocarbons by setting our taxes on these products at the same level as in the UK, this is unlikely to happen because of the broad interests of the Irish state.

There are, however, other administrative matters in respect of which the absurdities of a land border across two parts of the province of Ulster could be greatly mitigated. However different the administrative arrangements for the two health services may be, it should be possible to make both of them more readily accessible to people from either side of the border. The location and roles of hospitals in and close to the province of Ulster should clearly be decided by the two governments jointly so that whatever medical or surgical services people may need are made available to them as close to their homes as possible. Instead of being the back-end of two divided states, South Ulster – including for the purpose the county of Louth – should be treated for health purposes as a single region.

Many of these issues were not part of Una's own personal agenda for forgiveness and reconciliation between Irish people. But she was a sufficiently intelligent and informed peace activist to realise that economic development and political negotiation had essential roles to play in establishing a peaceful, reconciled and finally forgiving island of Ireland.

Making Rights Real

Making Connections and Owning Outcomes

Mary Robinson

In a work honouring Una O'Higgins O'Malley, with its apt title *Remembering to Forgive*, I believe I should follow her example and draw primarily on my own life experience in working for justice and human rights as essential components of authentic forgiveness and reconciliation. Una was herself well aware of this, as are many other contributors to this volume. Human rights are first and foremost about securing human dignity. I may add that such aspirational statements are important but the real test must be *implementation*, and I emphasise that energy and persistence are required, since this is no short-term endeavour. This brief paper then will concentrate on how to make rights real through the practice of participation. Many in this volume have been engaged in patient, meticulous and inclusive work to build alliances that connect the international, the regional and the local. The decision to test and learn how to make operational a rights-based approach at the very local level reflects commitment to, and growing understanding of, what is required to secure that human dignity. I believe such innovative work by communities here at home has an importance beyond the island of Ireland. Let me reinforce that message and encourage the continuance and development of the work for human rights not only in its own context and in that of forgiveness and reconciliation, but also to enable Una's admirers and successors to share and exchange their ideas and experiences with others on this island and throughout the world who have similar commitments.

The Globalisation Challenge and Human Rights

Failure to establish shared values and ethical standards in national and international decision-making is at the heart of the divides and controversy surrounding globalisation. We are increasingly divided between rich and poor. For many people, globalisation has come to mean vulnerability to unfamiliar, unaccountable and unpredictable forces that can bring on economic and social dislocation. Yet the international human rights framework is, or could be, a vital component and engine for promoting global values. Human rights have become the world's common benchmark for justice but have yet to become our common framework for action.

The Universal Declaration of Human Rights is the foundation of international human-rights law. It is the most important internationally agreed statement of values and shared responsibilities we have. Eleanor Roosevelt, who chaired the Human Rights Commission that drafted the declaration, urged that it must be written in simple language that could be understood 'in small places close to home'. The vision of the drafters was that everyone would share a common birthright and be engaged in promoting knowledge about it. It was proclaimed by the General Assembly of the United Nations in Paris on 10 December 1948 as a common standard of achievement for all peoples and all nations, to the end that every individual and every organ of society, keeping this declaration constantly in mind, shall strive by teaching and education to promote respect for those rights and freedoms. Yet it is still largely unknown in many parts of the world, including not just the poorest countries but also Ireland, Europe and the United States. In a world so deeply divided between rich and poor, North and South, religious and secular, us and them, we need more than ever the common values of the universal declaration. And we, civil society, including the business sector, need tools to hold governments accountable for their performance. The universal declaration, which has been affirmed and reaffirmed by governments for over half a century, is central to that cause. In a famous passage, Eleanor Roosevelt spelt out how she thought the message of human rights would be promoted in a world recently devastated by two terrible wars and a holocaust:

Where, after all, do universal human rights begin? In small places, close to home – so close and so small that they cannot be seen on any maps of the world. Yet they are the world of the individual person; the neighbourhood he lives in; the school or college he attends; the factory, farm, or office where he works. Such are the places where every man, woman, and child seeks equal justice, equal opportunity, equal dignity without discrimination. Unless these rights have meaning there, they have little meaning anywhere. Without concerted citizen action to uphold them close to home, we shall look in vain for progress in the larger world.

Almost sixty years later, we need to build on her words and to recognise that if human rights are to be known about and to matter in small places all over the world, they must matter much more in local communities and in the corridors of power. In the twenty-first century that means they must matter not just in governments but in the boardrooms of major corporations, in local communities and also in a personal way through the goodwill and commitment of individuals world wide. I see my current job in Realizing Rights as contributing to this transformation of human-rights principles into action and doing my bit to make the principles of human rights clear and accessible around the world. I am often asked what is meant by taking a 'human-rights-based approach' to issues. I should start by saying that there is no simple one-size-fits-all formula. Let me lay out some of the basic elements of a human-rights-based approach to problem solving.

- The focus is on *human dignity* – issues must be addressed in such a way as to maintain and enhance a person's dignity. This, for example, challenges the problem-solving approach of doing things 'to' or 'for' people but requires that they be done 'with' and 'by' people.
- The focus is on the 'equal and inalienable rights of all members of the human family': this means that people cannot be treated as means to an end and that issues of personal identity – whether gender, colour, disability, sexual orientation, political opinion etc. – can never justify inequality.

- The focus is on rights, not needs. This means that people have a justifiable expectation that their basic rights to housing, health provision, education and personal security must be met and that people are elected or appointed to government office to fulfil those obligations. They have a right to question, and should be enabled to question, how these obligations are fulfilled.
- The focus is on *participation, empowerment* and *accountability*: this means that rights-bearers (all of us) develop the skills and capacity to assert our rights knowledgeably and with due respect for the rights of others. At the same time, those in positions of power learn how to exercise their power in ways that promote the rights of all and expect to be, and are, held to account accordingly.

These are the key principles that underlie a human-rights-based approach but of course this can all too easily be dismissed as grandiose language. What does it actually mean?

Well, let us take it at its most basic. In a time of great global insecurity, after the genocide and horrors of the gas chambers of the Second World War, the nations of the world came together in 1948 and proclaimed the Universal Declaration of Human Rights as 'a common standard of achievement for all peoples and all nations'. They, and all subsequent new members of the United Nations (now over 191 nations across the globe), reaffirmed over and over again that recognising the dignity inherent in every human being is the 'foundation of freedom, justice and peace'. From this declaration they drew up much more detailed statements about the rights that states needed to protect and promote – the right to life, the right to due process, the right not to be ill treated, the right to an adequate income, the right to housing and education. In due course, they also drew up detailed documents that could almost be described as 'social contracts' around the rights of women, of racial minorities, of children, and they have just concluded a new convention on the protection and promotion of the rights of people with disabilities.

Of course, we all know that what governments say to other governments in the corridors of New York or Geneva does not necessarily reflect the reality on the ground. It is one thing to commit oneself in front of the international diplomatic community to respect the rights of all of one's citizens but who is going to make sure that this does, in fact, happen if not the citizens themselves? This is where the human-rights approach really starts to 'bite'. The powerless can always approach the powerful (and indeed often have felt that they had to do so) with pleas for generosity or requests that influence be exercised on their behalf. In the short term, this is a very understandable tactic – but long term it leaves the unequal power relationship unchallenged and indeed strengthened.

Rights and Needs

Compare the difference between the two following simple claims: 'I need a roof over my head' or 'I have a basic right to have a roof over my head'. The first claim is simply a statement of fact: it initiates no action; it imposes no responsibility on anyone to do anything about the person who has no roof over their head. If anything, it may even suggest that the problem lies with the person who needs the roof – 'If you need a roof over your head, what did you do to become homeless?' 'Why will Travellers not live like settled people in the public housing provided?' 'Do you think your need is greater than anyone else's?' The second statement, 'I have a basic right to a roof over my head,' conveys a totally different meaning. A 'right' on the part of one person automatically imposes a duty on someone else. So if I have a right to something, someone else has a corresponding duty. The government has already committed itself – to me, to society in general and to the international community – to respect everyone's right to a roof over their head. It has committed itself to do this in a nondiscriminatory way. And it has committed itself to ensure that this right is fully respected 'to the maximum of its available resources'. This means that the power relationship is dramatically changed. I, as a rights-bearer, am perhaps part of the problem but am also very much now part of the solution! In asserting my right, I am trying to address my need but I am also holding government to account and requiring that they comply with their duty to meet the needs of others and myself. I am making it clear that the problem is not my problem alone but a shared problem for society, since it is society that has recognised that all human beings should be treated with dignity, that they are equal and that they have rights, including the right to shelter.

Accordingly, if there is a problem with individuals not having adequate housing, this is no longer a challenge for them but for society as a whole to ensure that the appropriate legislation, policies and resources are in place to comply with this duty. In this way, the grandiose statements made in Geneva or New York start to have an impact on the lives of individuals. 'International human-rights law' can be an intimidating concept but in essence all it means is that the promises government make at the international level to uphold human rights can be used by people locally to bring about national and local change. Indeed, if people and their advocates do not insist on these promises being kept, international human-rights law is not worth the paper it is written on. When anyone phones the local council and asks what criteria they use for deciding which streets to clean and why her street has not been cleaned but other parts of town appear to be cleaned more regularly, and talks about the rights of herself and her community to have a safe environment in which children can play and which is not discriminated against, she is taking a human-rights-based approach. Such people are demanding accountability, transparency and equality of treatment. They are asserting that they and their community have rights that impose consequent duties on the public authority. I am not saying that they should not also phone their local TD or MLA and ask them to intervene on their behalf but, in the longer term, the challenge is surely to be listened to directly rather than to have to engage people to intervene on their behalf. The challenge for the elected representative is to facilitate and support that intervention to help people get a result.

When a community group involved in human-rights advocacy has its funding cut, it should ask on what criteria that decision has been taken, or how this decision conforms to the commitments made in government policy and international fora to tackle poverty and social exclusion, or whether the groups most affected were part of the decision-making process. This is a human-rights-based approach. To ask how this decision complies with particular commitments made under UN poverty-reduction strategies, or undermines pledges made to UN treaty bodies, or runs counter to domestic legislation or stated government policies, also means taking a human-rights-based approach. This approach places the 'burden of proof' on the policy maker. They are being required to justify their decision and justify that decision on grounds of fairness and equality. They can no longer claim that there is 'no more' funding. Where was the funding transferred to? Who made the decision to allocate money to some things and not others? On what criteria were the decisions made? Human rights impose standards of transparency and accountability and these are the tools that can be used to challenge decisions, frame responses and campaign for change. When issues raised by local women's groups – who are the conduit for voice and change – are ignored and dismissed and they fight back arguing about the discriminatory impact of particular policies, this is taking a rights-based approach. To marshal the overwhelming information and data that show how women are on the receiving end of poverty and exclusion is taking a rights-based approach because it places the concept of equality and nondiscrimination at the heart of such work.

Human Rights and Power
This is, of course, just the beginning, gathering information about needs on the ground. But then one must examine the standards the government has agreed upon regarding women. The Irish and British governments have both frequently stated their intention to target the exclusion of women and have introduced policies that are meant to do this. Holding them to account is taking a rights-based approach. Essential to this approach is working with others in developing campaigning strategies that

- define those needs as rights
- set indicators for change that will realise the particular rights
- define outcomes and results against the measurement of what makes the right real.

This is what is necessary to implement the international commitments made by government. The burden of proof is being shifted from the excluded and marginalised to government. Developing methods and processes within your local and national communities that allow the most excluded to voice the detail of their daily humiliation, and having them transform that exclusion into indicators of change, will make the rights guaranteed all human beings in the Universal Declaration of Human Rights almost sixty years ago real. The main source of opposition to this way of doing business is power – the vested interests of existing power that wishes to keep its power. The resistance by elected and administrative power to allocate resources in the ways required by government's international human-rights obligations reflects these vested interests.

Connecting human-rights indicators, set locally and in a participative process, will allow the intended beneficiaries of particular policies to measure change and hold those in authority accountable. And access and effective campaigning to ensure that resources are directed at meeting those indicators will reveal the vested interests and so require the 'fulfilling of respect' spelt out in the UN poverty-reduction strategies. Shaping and demanding transparent and accountable decision-making processes – processes already signed up to internationally by government – is the hard stuff of change. But without this, how can one change the allocation of resources and make real governments' lofty commitments to ending poverty and exclusion? The disconnect between the commitments signed up to at international level and the growing exclusion and disillusionment of those who are entitled to have those commitments made real in their lives is a dangerous democratic deficit, both at the nation-state level and for the international community. That disconnect can be measured here and elsewhere in hard statistics that bleakly spell out the widening gaps between the rich and the poor, the insider and the outsider. The disconnect between the current economic model of globalisation and the international human-rights framework is equally dangerous. Definitions of competitiveness that exclude the human and the social are, in my view, unproductive and unsustainable. Such definitions are often arrived at behind closed doors either in trade and treaty agreements or by the actions of multinational capital, e.g. in the growing privatisation of public services. They engender disillusionment and lack of trust that is profoundly unstable for economic and democratic growth.

I believe strongly that the ordinary citizen must be empowered and enabled to hold such exercises of power accountable through the nation-state government. Those governments must be challenged by their citizens to make integral the connection between the human-rights framework and global commitments on trade and competitiveness. 'Making connections and owning outcomes' helps to focus on working out how to use these tools of a human-rights approach to monitor how power is exercised to obtain results and change for those who need it. This includes the need for international linkages and networks such as a wonderful network of organisations and individuals developing strategies on economic and social rights: www.escr.net. The models, lessons and ideas coming from all this will help shape the current debates and interventions on globalisation that are taking place. All of us are 'learning by doing'. It is essential that we exchange and learn from each other and ensure that such knowledge and understanding can be transferred globally as well as in the shadow of broader political debates on this island. With this human-rights approach as a basic structure of local empowerment in Ireland as elsewhere, the prospects for social and political peace, reconciliation and forgiveness in Ireland and around the world – for which Una O'Higgins O'Malley spent her life's energies – become more feasible for all of us.

The Courts and Forgiveness

Kevin O'Higgins

IT IS HARDLY SURPRISING that forgiveness was one of the most important themes in the life of Una O'Higgins O'Malley. After all, her father, Kevin O'Higgins, forgave his killers as he lay dying. As a young child Una was deprived of her father but she succeeded in reconciling with the son of one of her father's killers, sharing with him the Sacrament of the Eucharist at a commemorative Mass in Booterstown. She also had a passionate interest in prison reform. Her deep concern for the integrity and accountability of the gardaí was one of the main reasons for her standing as an independent candidate in the general election of 1977. The latter two interests owed more to her paternity than to her apprenticeship in the distinguished firm of Arthur Cox and Company, which is hardly renowned for the practice of criminal law. Her interest in prison reform was, no doubt, influenced by many individuals that she encountered in her own personal journey to reconciliation. In this short tribute to my cousin and very generous godmother, rather than touch on the topics of prison reform or garda accountability (either of which might appear to be of more immediate interest to a judge), I wish to make some brief observations on the relative inability of the courts to encompass the concept of forgiveness in the areas of family law and criminal law in Ireland.

Apart from the natural feelings of anger, failure, sadness and anxiety caused by the breakdown of a marriage, the court proceedings are a source of considerable additional stress, even where there are sufficient assets to provide for the financial needs of the parties and their children. The experience of being in the same room as the spouse when the break-up of the marriage has been acrimonious, the hearing of evidence on intimate matters where such evidence is perceived to be unfair, slanted or downright false, together with feelings of uncertainty about the outcome, all add to the strain. However, even if the case is decided to the relative satisfaction of the parties, many litigants leave court with a feeling that they have not had an opportunity to articulate the sense of hurt and wrong that they have experienced and that their sense of grievance has been ignored. There are at least two reasons for this. First, although the relevant statutory provisions oblige the court to have regard to the conduct of the parties 'where it would be unjust not to do so', the conduct must be 'gross and obvious' before the court will be permitted to take it into account. For example, the fact that one of the parties had an affair (or even affairs) in the course of the marriage is unlikely to constitute the type of conduct contemplated by the statutory provisions as interpreted by the Supreme Court. The second reason is more fundamental and arises from the very nature of the hearing itself. It is sometimes very hard for the parties to understand the limitations of the legal process itself. Even the fairest hearing and most just decision – although clearly important and helpful to the parties – cannot seriously address the emotional and psychological issues involved in marriage breakdown. Acceptance, understanding and forgiveness are not within the gift of courts – they are matters for the parties themselves. The court cannot grant forgiveness nor decree reconciliation. Our law provides for advice to the parties in a marriage breakdown on the availability of mediation. In my experience, where mediation has been tried, even without success, the court hearing thereafter is usually less bitter and fraught than in cases where mediation has not been attempted. In some countries such as Canada the law makes formal provision for judicial mediation and those that support the idea are very enthusiastic about its merits. Even in our system there are times that a family law judge acts as a quasi-mediator. At least on some occasions, some low-key judicial intervention in the form of general comments on the issues involved may help the parties in settling the case. Comments by the judge at the end of the case may also offer some encouragement to the parties. Unfortunately, it is not possible for the court to deal with the human emotional and psychological issues that arise in family law cases and it is unrealistic to expect otherwise. However, a skilful, understanding and sympathetic family lawyer (perhaps especially a good solicitor) can have a huge influence in guiding and helping a litigant, not only through the court process, but also through the human crisis incurred following marital breakdown. In my view, the courts should only be used as a last resort. First, a solution imposed by a court is less satisfactory than one agreed freely by the parties. Second, the nature of the court process is such that it cannot deal with important human aspects of marriage breakdown and, third, the parties are saved the expense and strain inherent in court proceedings.

The concept of forgiveness is really peripheral to the criminal law. I suppose it could be argued that the application of the Probation Act 'without proceeding to a conviction' could be classified as a type of forgiveness but in the normal run of the criminal law, although the courts may show leniency in any given case, they are not in the business of forgiveness. It is sometimes difficult for the victims of crime to realise that the transaction in a criminal prosecution is between the People and the accused and not between the victim of crime and the accused. It is hard also for the victims of crime to appreciate that the impact of the crime on them is only one of many factors to be taken into account in the sentencing process. It is not unheard of for victim-impact reports to link the recovery of the victim with the length of sentence to be imposed. It is, of course, quite legitimate and understandable for a victim of a crime to feel that a particular offence demands a heavy sentence, both to mark its gravity and for his or her safety and that of others. Likewise, the forgiveness of the offender by the victim is only one of many factors to be taken into account by a sentencing judge. However, it is not often encountered in the court process. More usually the conviction of an accused, especially for serious crimes of violence, is greeted with raw emotions on the part of the victim's supporters.

Sometime around 1970, as a young barrister, I was involved in a murder case. The accused, the victim and the witnesses were all from the centre of Dublin, where the offence – a fatal stabbing – occurred. The trial

87

took place in the great forensic theatre of Green Street. The courthouse was full of family, friends and supporters of the dead young man. When the jury found the accused guilty of murder, the verdict was greeted with whooping, cheering and applause. The crowd went away satisfied. The convicted man and a few family members huddled together, weeping, before he was brought down to the cells to commence a life sentence. Over thirty-five years later the scene remains a vivid memory, probably because I was so unaccustomed to such a spectacle and I found it quite shocking. Yet such scenes are by no means uncommon. After all, is it not perfectly natural for the relatives and friends of somebody injured (or even killed) by the criminal acts of another to rejoice at the conviction and punishment of the perpetrator? For the cheering family and friends of the victim, the conviction and sentence of my client meant at least some form of redress for the hurt inflicted on them. Not surprisingly, forgiveness was absent from the scene in Green Street. When forgiveness occurs in a forensic setting, it can transform the whole proceedings. It is invariably moving.

Not long after this scene in Green Street, I was involved in another case where a young man was stabbed to death. The victim and his killer were very close friends and shared the same workplace. They had a trivial dispute during the day and determined to sort out the issue by having a fight after work. With several of their workmates looking on, the two young men – boys really – began to circle each other and to fight. After a few minutes one of them, who appeared to be getting the worst of things, produced a knife. The other lad was stabbed and brought off in an ambulance to hospital, where he died. His mate was arrested and brought away in a garda patrol car, sobbing. On the morning of the trial, the lobby outside the court was crowded with jurors, witnesses and gardaí, as well as solicitors and barristers. I was talking to the investigating sergeant, a veteran detective from Kerry. He pointed out to me a tense-looking couple in their mid-forties. These were the parents of the dead youth. A short time later he gestured towards another man and woman of similar age to the first couple. They, too, looked tense and anxious. The detective told me that he intended to introduce the two sets of parents to each other. I was aghast at the idea because I was sure that it would cause further trouble. In vain I tried to dissuade him from his course of action. Bewigged and begowned I might be, but he was old enough to be my father. I watched as he brought the parents of the dead boy to a relatively quiet corner of the lobby. He spoke to them and then left the sad couple for a few moments. He then came back with the other parents and introduced the two sets of parents to each other. They stiffened, hesitated, looked hard and then they all embraced, consoling each other in their shared but different anguish. I later asked the detective how he was so sure that things would work out as they had. 'I wasn't sure at all,' he said, ' but I thought the parents of the dead young lad might be able to forgive.' This incident remains with me not only for the shrewdness and wisdom of the veteran detective, but also as a vivid illustration of the liberating power of forgiveness, which was a theme close to Una's heart.

Diplomacy and Conflict

Noel Dorr

> And in the evening the oppression lifted,
> The hills came into focus; it had rained.
> Across the lawns and cultured flowers drifted,
> The conversation of the highly trained.

It was a warm afternoon in May 1980. It had rained earlier in the day but the rain had now cleared. We were in the Villa Madama, a seventeenth-century palazzo with ornate gardens on the Monte Mario, a suburb on a hill overlooking Rome. I was there with a friend and colleague from the Department of Foreign Affairs in Dublin, Padraig MacKernan (later ambassador to Paris and secretary of the department), to represent Ireland at a meeting of senior EU officials. We met monthly as the Political Committee and reported to foreign ministers. Our task was, where possible, to coordinate the foreign policy positions of the EU member states on major international issues. We were in Rome because Italy now held the six-month presidency in succession to Ireland.

The meeting was slow to start. The Italian presidency, we were told, was still working on a draft for a common EU policy statement on the Middle East, where the Israeli-Palestinian conflict was flaring up again. So we walked in the ornate gardens after the rain had cleared. The drivers of the embassy cars that had brought us all there waited outside.

> The gardeners watched them pass and priced their shoes,
> The chauffeurs waited, reading in the drive

For them to finish their exchange of views.
It seemed the image of the private life.

As we walked and talked we passed our British colleague, who was sitting on a seat in the garden reading his papers. He looked up and murmured 'the conversation of the highly trained'. Intrigued, we wondered at the reference. Just then we were called into the meeting in the villa so we had no time to ask.

Four months later, I had taken up a new post in New York as Irish Permanent Representative – which is to say ambassador – to the United Nations. My colleague, who had succeeded me in Dublin, came out for the opening weeks of the UN General Assembly session. When we met, he presented me with a copy of *The Collected Works of W.H. Auden,* inscribed 'In memory of an afternoon in the Villa Madama in May 1980'. I read the whole thirteen-line poem then and I have read it many times since. It was written in 1939 as a description of a diplomatic negotiation. The final five lines explain what hung in the balance:

> Far off, no matter what good they intended,
> The armies waited for a verbal error,
> And on the issue of their charm depended,
> A land laid waste, and all its young men slain,
> The women weeping and the towns in terror.

The EU statement that we eventually drafted that day in Rome was less momentous than the negotiation depicted by Auden and it did little to settle the conflict in the Middle East, a thousand miles away, which has grown worse, not better, since then. But that Auden poem has remained with me, with its image of armies waiting and ready to attack. I know of no better justification for some of the more wearying aspects of diplomacy than the thought that negotiation skilfully conducted, and words put together well and carefully, may, on occasion, avert the horrors of war – or end a conflict where women weep over young men and towns live in terror.

The editor of the present volume has chosen remembrance and forgiveness as the best reflection of the life and work of Una O'Higgins

O'Malley. But I do not think that diplomacy in its best sense – that of dialogue with 'the other', directed to understanding and averting conflict – would be too far from her concerns. Diplomacy of a kind must have existed from earliest times. Human groups – tribes, peoples, kingdoms – came into contact with each other and developed channels for organised contact that gradually helped to soften initial hostility and suspicion. In antiquity, diplomacy in the Middle East involved sporadic contact at most between separate kingdoms over issues of trade or tribute. The cuneiform tablets of Tell el Amarna written in Aramaic, the international language of the era in that region, show exchanges of this kind between the Egyptian pharaoh and the king of the Hittites in the fourteenth century BC. In classical Greece, heralds were under the protection of Hermes, messenger of Zeus, and Greek city-states sent envoys skilled in rhetoric to present their case before decision-making councils or assemblies of citizens of other city-states. The cities of mediaeval and renaissance Italy were the first to develop a system of resident embassies and the rules and practices of diplomacy in the modern era can be traced back to the emergence in seventeenth-century Europe after the Thirty Years' War of an international system based on recognition by each state of the sovereign independence of every other in the system. The best kind of diplomacy, as I see it, is directed to the averting or settlement of conflict. But diplomacy has other aspects, not all of them equally benign. States and rulers have always seen diplomacy, legitimately enough, as directed to the promotion of their interests in dealings with other states. But, on occasion, more ominously, diplomatic exchanges have been a prelude to war, most often of the strong against the weak.

Thucydides, in the fifth century BC, tells us of the arguments presented to Melos by Athenian envoys sent to persuade that city to ally itself with Athens in its war against Sparta. 'You know as well as we do,' they told the Melian assembly, 'that … the strong do what they have the power to do and the weak accept what they must.' The Melians declined the invitation and maintained their neutrality – to their cost: the Athenians took the city, killed its men and sold women and children into slavery. In modern times, another realist, von Clausewitz, saw a continuity between diplomacy and war. War for him was 'not merely a political act, but also a real political instrument, a continuation of political commerce, a carrying out of the same by other means'. For most of us today, war is seen as a failure, and not as an extension, of diplomacy. And if, as Cicero said, *silent enim leges inter arma* (In times of war, the law falls silent) then when great wars end it again becomes the task of diplomacy to reconstruct a shattered international system.

In eighteenth- and nineteenth-century Europe, statesmen and diplomats acting for their sovereigns bargained and traded territorial gains on the map after major wars. But as they did so, they also began slowly to develop a sense of their responsibility to seek peace and stability through the post-war settlements that they made – what one of the documents at the Peace of Utrecht of 1713 called *securitas et tranquillitas Europae* or, as the French termed it, *le repos de l'Europe*. At the Congress of Vienna at the end of the Napoleonic Wars in 1815, 'the bartering of people about', as Woodrow Wilson called it later, was still in evidence. But as they redrew the map of Europe and jostled, as in the past, for individual advantage for their countries, the representatives of the major powers who were the architects of the settlement also showed some sense of what has been called 'system consciousness'. For all the limitations and self-interest of the agreements they reached, they were becoming aware, even more than their predecessors, that they had a common responsibility for the future peace of Europe. They exercised that responsibility several times in the first half of the nineteenth century by meeting at conferences and settling international disputes in ways that fell short of further large-scale war.

The disaster of the First World War was widely blamed on the failure of this older kind of diplomacy that had staked so much on the maintenance of an increasingly precarious 'balance of power' between the great European powers. US president Woodrow Wilson, a man of moral purpose, impressed on the victorious Allies the need for a radically new approach in international relations – what he called 'a community of power' rather than a shifting and changing 'balance'. Under pressure from Wilson, the other Allies agreed at the Versailles Peace Conference of 1919 to create a League of Nations – a new, standing, 'collective security' organisation of states, committed to principles set out in a covenant that all of its members agreed to abide by. This was the first attempt to put into practice an idea that had been advocated at various times over the centuries by writers and thinkers such as William Penn, the Abbé de St Pierre and Immanuel Kant. The league was a wholly new departure in diplomacy. It was a standing international organisation based on the principle that states shared a common responsibility for the maintenance of peace and order in the international system and its covenant became, if only to a limited degree, a kind of recognised 'constitution' for international society. Una O'Higgins O'Malley's father was a member of the Irish government that applied for membership of the league in 1923 and he served as a member of the Irish delegation to the League Assembly in 1926.

The league had some achievements to its credit in the 1920s but in face of the rise of totalitarian regimes in the 1930s it faltered and then virtually disintegrated, despite the heroic efforts of an Irishman, Sean Lester, the acting secretary-general in Geneva, to hold it together during the Second World War. But notwithstanding the apparent failure of this first attempt to establish such an organisation, the concept remained alive through the darkest years of that war – the most destructive in history – and the Allied leaders agreed, even before the fighting stopped, to set up in its place a new collective security organisation – the United Nations. The membership of the new organisation was limited at first and nearly a decade passed before Ireland and several other states that had not been belligerents were allowed to join. As the great decolonisation movement worked itself out in the post-war years, however, scores of new states emerged to independence. In effect, through the second half of the twentieth century, humankind reorganised itself into a world of sovereign states. The first international act of each new state in turn after it became independent was to look for UN membership and, as a result, the United Nations in our day has long outgrown its birth in 1945 as a continuation of the wartime alliance. It has now become a universal organisation of states, the first such organisation in human history.

The UN is now more than sixty years old. It is weak and fragile in many respects – and often ineffectual. But for all its faults and weaknesses, it is also, I believe, indispensable in a world where, as Kofi Annan put it in the millennium year, 'In addition to the separate responsibilities each state bears towards its own society, states are, collectively, the custodians of our common life on this planet'. I do not see how the nearly two hundred sovereign states in the world today can exercise that role unless they do it by close cooperation through the network of international organisations, with the United Nations at its centre, which has been developed since the Second World War. The most important aspect of the United Nations, however, is that all of the world's nearly two hundred states have come, formally at least, to accept the charter, its foundation document, as a statement of fundamental principles to govern international relations. The charter is in need of some adaptation. But it is a document imbued with a kind of moral purpose that is wholly new in the long, amoral and often bloody history of international relations. This is evident from its preamble in which 'We, the peoples of the United Nations' express a determination

- 'to save succeeding generations from the scourge of war which twice in our lifetime has brought untold sorrow to mankind …
- to reaffirm faith in fundamental human rights, in the dignity and worth of the human person, in the equal rights of men and women, and of nations large and small …
- to promote social progress and better standards of life in larger freedom …
- and, for these ends, to practice tolerance and live together in peace with one another as good neighbours.'

I venture to suggest that these aims, set out in the charter and now adopted, in principle at least, by nations spanning all the world's cultures, deserve to be mentioned in a volume that reflects the particular concerns of Una O'Higgins O'Malley in its title, *Remembering to Forgive*. Diplomacy has many aspects – bilateral and multilateral – and at one time or another, during a career spanning four decades, I have found myself involved on behalf of Ireland in some of these. Three stand out in my mind as areas with a particular bearing on the concept that I have been concerned with here – that is, diplomacy as an effort to avert or end conflict. I will conclude here with some brief memories that draw on that involvement.

My first such memory is of the seemingly mundane work of helping to draft treaties that, by building cumulatively on older treaties, have created the European Union of today. I say mundane because in such negotiations, as in the daily work of the union, Irish representatives, like those of all other member states, show a pragmatic concern for national interest. But mixed with that, though not always in evidence at each meeting, are glimpses of a larger vision – the continuing development of what John Hume has called the world's greatest peace process. *Securitas et tranquillitas Europae* was an aim that statesmen and diplomats vainly strove for in an earlier era. It has been largely achieved in our time and this continent, which for centuries was the region where the world's great conflicts began, has evolved a new kind of relationship between its states and its diverse peoples. The result is a union of states and peoples committed to democracy and human rights. This is an international structure of a wholly new kind that could, and should, play an important role in the achievement of a larger, and still elusive, aim – the creation, over time, of a world of peace, of order and of justice. A second area of diplomacy in which I have found myself has been the United Nations. So much will be evident from the emphasis I have given to it. I will limit myself here to a single memory from those years.

It was a Saturday night, turning into Sunday morning, 1 August 1982. At 2 a.m. I took a phone call, sitting sleepily on the edge of the bed in my apartment in New York. It was the Lebanese ambassador. He told me that his country's capital Beirut, which had been under siege for weeks by Israeli forces at war with the PLO, had come under extremely heavy bombardment during the night with much loss of life and destruction. He told me that he had instructions from his government to demand an immediate meeting of the Security Council. I knew, sleepy as I was, that the responsibility for calling and chairing such a meeting had passed to Ireland, in monthly rotation, at midnight, just two hours before. We did meet eventually at 8.30 a.m. on Sunday morning. And, after much intensive negotiation, the fifteen-member council, later that day, unanimously adopted a resolution that demanded a ceasefire and authorised the secretary-general to deploy UN observers around Beirut. The UN was unable to deploy its observers at that point and the resolution did not bring an immediate end to the fighting, although it became part of a framework that, eventually, with the departure of the PLO and the lifting of the Israeli siege, brought respite, and peace of a sort, to Lebanon. But now, in memory, I link our fraught and intense negotiations on that Sunday in New York with those described in the Auden poem quoted earlier.

I will briefly mention a third and final area. It is one that was directly related to the concerns that animated and shaped so much of Una O'Higgins O'Malley's life and that had its counterpart in her own work and that of many others. I mean the effort through negotiation, over several decades and at various levels, to achieve peace and reconciliation – in Northern Ireland, in the island of Ireland and between Britain and Ireland. I remember attending the Sunningdale Conference as an official in 1973: it deserved to succeed but didn't. I remember my time in London in the 1980s: the eighteen months of intensive negotiation involving political leaders and officials on both sides that prepared the way for the Anglo-Irish Agreement of 1985. And I remember the effort to report home with absolute accuracy and objectivity to taoiseach and ministers on the positions of the prime minister and government in London during that period. I remember too the careful drafting and redrafting of documents at that time, and again of quite different documents in the early 1990s, all of which helped to prepare the way for the peace process and the Belfast Agreement of 1998. Words then were, and still are, of importance, and there was no room for the 'verbal error' to which Auden referred. But, as we have seen since, though words may stay conflict they must be supported by action if there is to be true peace. Finally, and most personally, I remember visiting hospitals in the mid-1980s – to see those injured by the bomb at Harrod's in 1983 and the Brighton bomb in 1985; and I remember the four or five people I met later, at different times: people who had suffered either personal injury or grievous loss, or both, when the Grand Hotel in Brighton collapsed in the explosion. They, like so many others in Britain and Ireland who suffered in those times, will always remember what happened. I hope that, like Una O'Higgins O'Malley, they will also find it possible to forgive.

The Other Superpower

Dervla Murphy

First they ignore you. Then they laugh at you. Then they attack you. Then you win.

Mahatma Gandhi

On 15 February 2003, millions took to the streets in hundreds of cities and towns all over the world to protest against the invasion of Iraq. Representatives of every age group, every profession and social class, every race and religion turned out, their common slogan 'The World Says NO to War!' Most had never before demonstrated for or against anything, yet now they made history: those demos were the largest ever seen. And, where opinion polls were run, national majorities backed the marchers. In *The New York Times* on 17 February, Patrick Tyler wrote of 'two superpowers on the planet: the United States and world public opinion'. Two months later, Kofi Annan also described the global antiwar movement as 'the other superpower' – somewhat OTT, one might think, given Washington's indifference to world public opinion. However, that indifference was not total. Such worldwide support for the rule of law, and for more Hans Blix-led 'jaw-jaw', made waves in the White House. This moral pressure, so passionately yet quietly exerted on all continents, sent the Bush administration (against its hardliners' inclinations) back to the Security Council. But again, as in November 2002, Washington was stymied. Six non-permanent members (Angola, Cameroon, Chile, Guinea, Mexico and Pakistan, all to some extent dependent on the US) lined up to deny their overlord UN authority for a blatant violation of its own charter, an unprovoked attack on a sovereign state. For months US envoys had been touring those countries, muttering threats; undoubtedly the other superpower's influence strengthened their governments' refusal to be cowed. When it became clear that Washington's proposed resolution would be defeated, it was hastily withdrawn. The invasion then went ahead, inflicting on Iraq a state of anarchy that, halfway through its fourth year, becomes bloodier by the day.

Immanuel Wallerstein, author of the three-volume *Modern World-System,* notes that this was 'the first time since the UN was founded that the US, on an issue that mattered to it, could not get a majority on the Security Council'. It is small consolation to the Iraqis that the other superpower thus helped politically to humiliate 'the biggest bully on the block' (Colin Powell's admiring description of his own country). However, that Security Council rebellion has done something, over time, to counter the Goebbels-style propaganda blitz launched in the US during the autumn of 2002. Also, it starkly exposed to the whole world the US's contempt for the UN – not a new phenomenon but in March 2003 Washington's last withered fig leaf fell away. Since then, all those grotesque claims to be the leading exporter of democracy, stability, justice and peace have increasingly provoked angry ridicule. In *A Peaceful Superpower,* David Cortright shrewdly points out that 'The US administration … could not be seen as preparing to take over the Iraqi state … To maintain the deceit that was necessary to justify military action, Washington short-circuited preparations for the war's aftermath'. Post-invasion, antiwar groups persistently challenged that deceit, their task made easier by Paul Wolfowitz, then US deputy defence secretary. Incautiously, he admitted to a *Vanity Fair* interviewer (9 May 2003), 'The truth is that for reasons that have a lot to do with US government bureaucracy, we settled on the one issue that everyone could agree on, which was weapons of mass destruction as the core reason'.

Ireland's joining NATO's tendentiously named Partnership for Peace in November 1999 ended all those tiresome arguments about our amorphous neutrality. Now, like it or not, we belong to a military alliance dedicated to making the world safe for oil pipelines and free marketeers. The bonds between Capitalism Rampant and Militarism Unbound are long established and strong – and getting stronger. In 2003, when many outraged citizens denounced the Irish government's collaboration with the US Air Force, we were ignored. The Celtic Tiger being an animal fed by the invaders of Iraq, any moral scruples about illegal regime change would seriously threaten its food supply. In exchange for continuing affluence, we must support Militarism Unbound. We are also contributing our mite to the worldwide spread of sophisticated weaponry. (A list of the industries making components for 'defence' clients may be obtained from AFrI, 16 Harcourt Street, Dublin 2.) Demands from the other superpower's Irish contingent for this particular dish to be removed from the Celtic Tiger's menu prompt the predictable explanation: if you're seeking a steady flow of inward investment, you can't pick and choose. However, weapons are not bought for their decorative value; one day they will be used to kill and maim indiscriminately. And on such an issue it is the government's responsibility to take action. One can't realistically expect individual Irish workers to turn down good jobs for so abstract a reason (abstract if you live far from all war zones). They can argue, plausibly enough, 'What difference would it make, banning them in Ireland? Someone else, somewhere else, would gladly manufacture all those components'. This echoes the arms-dealers' favourite defence – but imagine a drugs dealer explaining in a court of law, 'I sold the heroin because if I didn't, someone else would, and why shouldn't I have the profit?' There is a telling dichotomy here. It is not illegal, or commonly regarded as immoral, for Minority World governments to sell vast quantities of armaments, including DU-tipped shells and cluster bombs, to any tyrannical regime that will pay for them. Yet to deal in drugs, which are not nearly so harmful to so many, is illegal and commonly regarded as immoral. The military-industrial complex rules OK.

In August 2006 Michael Ahern, Minister for Trade and Commerce, announced that 'new legislation on strategic export controls' would soon come before the Oireachtas. He added, 'I wish to emphasise that Ireland does not have an arms trade nor do we wish to promote one'. Three sentences later the minister explained, 'Licences for military exports from Ireland are granted in strict accordance with the EU Code of Conduct on Arms Exports'. So although we don't have an arms trade, we do grant licences for military exports. Witness another of the Celtic Tiger's circus tricks, a double somersault.

Since 9/11 military action has been vaunted as the only really effective protection against terrorism – never mind the hundreds of billions of dollars being spent annually in the US on grossly swollen counterterrorism agencies. And in 2006 we heard the first nervous whispers, in non-alarmist quarters, about the possibility of a Third World War. China, Russia and four Central Asian republics have formed the Shanghai Cooperation Organisation and invited India, Pakistan, Mongolia and Iran to join – just as the US is seeking UN support for a Teheran-punishing trade embargo. *The Boston Globe* has described this 'anti-Bush alliance' as a 'tectonic shift in geopolitics'. And Stephen F. Cohen, writing in *The Nation* (10 July 2006), warns that NATO's expansion 'has already brought US–Russian relations near breaking point without actually benefiting any nation's security'.

When the other superpower raised its banners on 15 February 2003, it could be seen that many people were very frightened and were protesting not only against the invasion of Iraq but also against the violence inherent in the 'New American Century', as visualised by Washington's neo-cons in the mid-nineties. Given the frankness of US military planners, it's a wonder we're not even more scared. In 1995 a US Strategic Command document asserted that the US must 'retain the right [sic] of first use of nuclear weapons', even against a non-nuclear signatory of the 1970 Nuclear Non-Proliferation Treaty. The US has also emasculated the 1972 Biological and Toxic Weapons Convention by refusing to accept verification inspections, ostensibly to protect the trade secrets of pharmaceutical and biotechnology companies. European bio-weapons experts are now worried that 'the US may have rejected the bio-weapons protocol because it is committed to continuing and expanding its secret programs'. In May 2003 the Rand Corporation warned that 'The potential for an accidental or unauthorised nuclear missile launch in

Russia or the US has grown over the past decade'. Most chilling of all, the Pentagon's solution to the problem of increasing majority world poverty was outlined in Vision for 2020, a Clinton-administration brochure issued by the Space Command. It foretells that by 2020 'the globalisation of the world economy' will have brought about 'a widening between haves and have-nots', leading to alienation. And this will prompt an increase in anti-US violence, probably including WMD-armed terrorists. Hence the need for 'full-spectrum dominance to protect US national interests and investments' by using 'space-based strike weapons enabling the application of precision force from, to, and through space'.

In 1995 Japanese officials were advised by the US Ballistic Missile Defense Organisation that 'Theater Missile Defense is the last military business opportunity for this century'. Soon after, the former German chancellor Gerhard Schroeder decided that Germany has a 'vital economic interest' in developing space technology. And so the military-industrial gravy train rolls smoothly on, only occasionally jarred when responsible scientists, not employed by the war industry, question the feasibility of BMD (aka Star Wars). The most terrifying feature of Vision for 2020 is its authors' readiness to control disorderly poor people by killing them. In 1990 one might have laughingly dismissed this 'vision' as the sick daydreaming of a few Pentagon psychopaths. But a lot has happened since then, both technically and politically. In 1992 we rejoiced to hear about 'the peace dividend', money that could now be diverted from armaments to more benign uses. But soon we realised that those who run the global economy have no interest in peace. Eisenhower's famous warning – 'avoid too close a relationship between the military and industry' – has been ignored for the past half-century and the military-industrial complex was not going to allow the end of the Cold War to reduce its profits. This partly explains NATO's rapid expansion when the Soviet Union was no more and the Warsaw Pact had disbanded. Another part of the explanation has to do with 'full-spectrum dominance'.

The open admiration for Hitler and Mussolini expressed during the 1930s in both the US and Britain was not as freakish as it has since been presented. In our own day, there are threatening resemblances between the fascist mindset and the militarist/free-market ideologies. While seeming to cultivate political correctness, many Minority World governments continue to practise to assume white/Caucasian superiority, from which follows the superior race's right to dominate the world. (In this context the Japanese are honorary whites, as they were in apartheid South Africa.) We find Hitler's methodical exterminations utterly incomprehensible – the ultimate evil, some say. Yet rampant capitalists are now treating millions of human beings with equal cruelty, using different methods. People were killed systematically in Hitler's concentration camps and gas chambers. Majority World people die of malnutrition and preventable diseases in a disorganised way – but still they die. Of course, rampant capitalists don't plan to kill people. They just let it happen – not a big difference from their victims' point of view. Meanwhile they feign concern: 'Make Poverty History' and such inane slogans are meant to hold their collective mask in place – a mask showing a third worried face. The other superpower needs to focus, steadily, on the hideous truth that the effects of Capitalism Rampant, guarded by Militarism Unbound, are more destructive than Hitler's death camps when spread out over time and space.

The poor are not poorer in 2006 than in 1970 only because of overpopulation, wars, famines, droughts or floods, or because their governments are corrupt or their workers lazy or their technologies backward or their cultures primitive. In pursuit of profit our world sustains many corrupt leaders, eliminates honest politicians unwilling to facilitate exploitative 'free' market operations, erects trade barriers to deprive hard workers of a fair reward for their labours, sacrifices countless small farmers on the altar of agribusiness, funds gigantic 'development projects' usually detrimental to the well-being of local populations, but hugely profitable for multinational construction companies. All those facts, though so well known, need to be often repeated. The Nazi killers and their non-German collaborators knew what they were doing. Can it be said that rampant capitalists know not what they do? Probably yes, in many cases – cases of 'intentional ignorance'. Their backgrounds, education and ambitions isolate them from most of their fellow men and women. They don't know what it feels like to be hungry, thirsty, too hot or too cold, or too wet to sleep because the roof is leaking. They sit in multistoreyed headquarters calculating how to organise the world for the benefit of the rich while trying to persuade everyone that eventually 'trickle-down' will benefit the poor. At quite frequent intervals they tour some Majority World district, their guides compliant local politicians and/or entrepreneurs, their base a five-star hotel. During 'humanitarian crises' they sometimes visit disaster areas and are photographed, looking suitably sombre, with the afflicted population and their foreign helpers. If International Monetary Fund (IMF) bureaucrats, deciding that a Structural Adjustment Program (SAP) was the best way forward for a deeply indebted country, could imagine the starvation, pain, grief and despair suffered by the poor as a direct result of that decision, would they persist in enforcing it? If they met children mentally underdeveloped for lack of adequate nourishment while their brains were developing because a SAP had stopped food subsidies, would they think again? Possibly. But then, why can they not visualise their decisions' results? Nobody is forcing them to wear blinkers. The facts are not hidden. Over the past few decades scores of writers, carefully documenting their evidence, have recorded the multiple hardships inflicted worldwide by Capitalism Rampant.

The World Bank, World Trade Organisation, IMF and various kindred institutions kill by remote control. Bluntly to state that fact invites accusations of paranoia. We have been conditioned to regard all such pillars of capitalism as respectable and well intentioned. To point out that the emperor has no clothes by identifying the harm they do can seem like a presumptuous attack on our whole way of life. After all, those institutions are often led by distinguished retired politicians or senior civil servants (Paul Wolfowitz is now president of the World Bank) and are staffed by high-powered international experts and advised by eminent professors taking a sabbatical to pick the sort of fruit not grown in the groves of academe. Such people must surely know what they're doing – to revile them merely exposes our own ignorance; we ordinary folk can't possibly understand high finance, trade agreements, 'defence' requirements and so on. Granted, undisguisable mistakes costing billions of dollars are occasionally made. And quite a few individuals or groups have been detected running corrupt rackets or subsidising vicious regimes. And of course it's a shame nobody seems able to do much about poverty. However, at numerous lavishly funded international conferences these rampant capitalists eloquently speak up for 'democracy' and 'human rights' and so far they have very successfully kept our own affluent show on the road. It's simply not on to argue that their cruel activities and arrogant attitudes foster a global atmosphere conducive to terrorism. Most Minority World citizens – busy about their own concerns, taking only a passing interest in distant places – are easy prey for those skilled PR manipulators who encourage us to view the root causes of increasing world poverty as dauntingly complex. To soothe the unease we frequently feel when disaster strikes yet again, we can sign a cheque (as the Irish do with record-breaking generosity) or collect truckloads of blankets, toys, clothes, tinned foods – donations too often surplus to requirements at their destinations. But as Vincent Browne has more than once reminded us, 'Injustice is not rectifiable by charity, it is rectifiable by justice.' Giving doesn't absolve us from the harder task of thinking about the most effective way to oppose rapacity. There's an urgent need to question doggedly the inner workings of Capitalism Rampant, refusing to be daunted by its apparent complexities. When the free market has been denuded of its euphemisms, we realise that there are in fact no complexities here; the profit motive is uncomplicated in its ruthless immorality.

The word 'consensus' used to have a wholesome ring about it. But not any more, not since the 'Washington Consensus' was proclaimed some thirty years ago, advocating the unimpeded flow of foreign money throughout the Majority World while allowing private investors legally to asset strip what had been public services. A sinister ploy, hugely enriching for comparatively few – but Nemesis may not be far away. The Washington Consensus enthused about 'liberalisation' and 'deregulation', weasel words suggesting enlightenment and tolerance. The 'free market' also sounds good – letting everyone with entrepreneurial talents off the leash to earn more and more, or anyway to acquire more and more, sometimes without the labour of earning. In this stimulating environment our Tiger grew fast, overtaking most of its European competitors, and an ominous number of Irish citizens adapted to 'the loan culture', as though living in debt were a human right. Then, gradually, more and more Minority World residents (recruits to the other superpower) began to question this blissfully liberated and deregulated paradise. How come Enron could happen? How come twenty-six hedge-fund managers each earned, in 2005, an average of $263 million, while one man, James Simon of Renaissance Technologies, scooped in $1.5 billion? Over the centuries, regulations have been seen as a necessary prop for civilised societies; deregulated human beings don't behave very well. It's therefore no surprise that lawlessness now menaces the financial world's stability.

That world's obfuscating jargon would seem comical were it not trying to conceal criminal activities. Collateralised debt obligations, market credit default swaps, split capital trusts – and who can explain 'credit derivative futures'? Not Gillian Tett, the *Financial Times'* capital-markets guru. Having attempted, unsuccessfully, to elucidate, she confessed to a gut feeling that the phenomenon is extremely dangerous. Warren Buffett, said to be the second richest man in the world, was no more explicit, describing 'credit derivatives' as 'financial weapons of mass destruction'. According to Gabriel Kolko, writing in *Spokesman 92*, 'Many of these innovative financial products exist in cyberspace only and often are simply tax dodges for the ultra-rich'. In *Safeguarding Financial Stability* by Gerry J. Schanisi, an IMP-sponsored book published in March 2006, we are assured that the Washington Consensus has generated 'tremendous private and social benefits'. But unfortunately, owing to 'the irrational development of global finance', there is now 'the potential (although not necessarily a high likelihood) for fragility, instability, systemic risk, and adverse economic consequences'. The IMF's managing director, Rodrigo de Rato, complained in May 2006 that too many 'financial adventurers' have been inventing too many 'new products' not open to the scrutiny of either national governments or international banks. He admitted to being deeply troubled by the recent weakening of the IMF's power to dictate the economic policies of Majority World governments; since 2003 the balance of trade can no longer be made consistently to benefit the Minority

World. The prices of certain crucially important commodities – chiefly petroleum, silver, copper, nickel, zinc – have doubled on the world market. In particular, all the oil-exporting countries have been gaining power since the mid-nineties and are much relishing their status as creditors to the US. Between 2001 and 2005, the value of the dollar against the euro declined by 28 per cent. In April 2006 Stephen Roach, Morgan Stanley's chief economist, foretold 'a major financial crisis' likely to flummox all the relevant institutions, including the World Bank and the IMF. Two months later he spoke of 'a certain sense of anarchy' that left the political and academic communities 'unable to explain the way the new world is working'. The Bank for International Settlements agreed with him. Its annual report considered, among numerous other worries, 'trends difficult to rationalise'.

Is Capitalism Rampant, in its present incarnation, soon to be felled by the goddess of retribution? If so, how can the other superpower help to thwart its reincarnation? To find the answer, read *One No, Many Yeses*, a truly inspiring book by an extraordinary young man. Paul Kingsnorth has lived on five continents with the other superpower's pioneers, the new revolutionaries (as far removed from communism as from capitalism) who have already been on the march for a decade or so. He writes: 'For these people – millions upon millions of them – globalisation is exclusion ... It is this exclusion which has created a rapidly rising popular movement, led by the poor in the "developing" lands and now developing in the rich world too.' Paul's immensely exciting book is not about what might be done or what should be done but about what is being done – in places most of us have never heard of – to reverse the requisitioning of public goods (in the widest sense of that term) for private gain.

As the global scene shifts, the hard bit for us Minority Worlders will be coming to terms, in our personal lives, with the uncomfortable (sometimes literally uncomfortable) fact that rectifying economic injustice means the 'haves' having less. Otherwise the 'have-nots' can't have *more*. You don't need to be any sort of 'expert' to recognise this reality. Justice won't be served by transnational corporations ostentatiously sponsoring 'good causes'. Or by fiddling with the structures of the world funk, IMF,

WTO et al. to make them seem less predatory. All those institutions must somehow be dismantled (maybe Nemesis will see to this?), leaving the global stage clear for the new revolutionaries. Each group can then organise its own economic activities in ways appropriate to its region's resources, skills and traditions. In the twenty-first (or twenty-second?) century, these groups will not, of course, be operating in isolation. Globalisation is irreversible. But it doesn't have to, nor can it, retain its present form; if it tries to, some version of Vision 2020 will inevitably come true.

Pessimists grimly foretell that the essential mind-shift (accepting that more for them means less for us) can only come about involuntarily and painfully through violent conflict – not, as the other superpower would wish, through an intellectual appreciation of our planet's limitations and the hubris of greed. Given the present distribution of power, economic and military, it's easy to see that argument. But even if the pessimists are proved right, one can look far ahead, beyond the cataclysm, to an era when the descendants of those 'millions and millions' of whom Paul Kingsnorth writes will inherit the earth – because they have the wits and the guts to live sanely. Ultimately numbers do count and the Minority World is just that, its current omnipotence a profoundly damaging aberration. Meanwhile, on our own feverishly affluent little island (too abruptly transformed from a cabbage patch to an industrial park), there is at least one reason for optimism. Young people formed a high percentage of those crowds who repeatedly protested at Shannon against official Ireland's subservience to Washington. The Celtic Tiger's cubs, if we register only their sordidly newsworthy activities, can seem an unpromising litter, much given to binge drinking, drug dealing, underage sex, dangerous driving and over-eating. Yet here, as elsewhere, many un-newsworthy youngsters are proud of belonging to the other superpower. They cleverly counter the mass media's dumbing-down efforts by exchanging internet information with the 'global resistance' movement. They are on guard against the machinations of Capitalism Rampant and Militarism Unbound. And they know that the 'Growth Society', as such, is doomed – not because its madness will eventually become apparent to its promoters but because it defies the laws of nature by assuming that finite resources are infinite. Individuals who suffer from comparable delusions are locked up for their own safety.

PART III
FORGIVING

Forgiveness

Padraig J. Daly

I
The hardest thing
Is to offer forgiveness
Where forgiveness is inconsequential.

And you reach out merely
To lance your own
Suppurating soul.

II
Caterpillars make themselves new
And fly,
Trees cover their wounds and thrive,
Skin sheds and mends
Septennially.

But what will repair
The unforgiven heart?

A Door to Lost Treasure

Colum Kenny

FORGIVENESS IS A KEY that opens the door to lost treasures. The treasures lie behind a wall built with bricks of pain, judgement and possessiveness. But for many of us forgiveness is not easy. Yet what do most of us have to forgive? Many of us are fortunate enough not to have suffered the immediate pain of some terrible crime or outrage. We are not an Una O'Higgins O'Malley who lost her parent to political assassins. We are not Jews or Rwandans who have witnessed our families wiped out by genocide. We are not the isolated victims of child abuse or rape. So forgiveness for most of us should be relatively easy. Why not then ask ourselves if there is any way in which we can exercise forgiveness in our own lives and thus test ourselves by trying to do so? The rewards are worth the effort. Do we harbour resentment? If we do, this fact is an indicator that someone may be in need of forgiveness by us or that, for our own sake, we need to forgive them in any event. How honest are we about acknowledging our resentment to ourselves? Some resentment is so deep-seated that it only emerges into our consciousness when we are helped by a third party such as a counsellor to see ourselves. But quite a lot of resentment is visible if we simply open our eyes and look. Unfortunately, because resentment is associated with pain, we tend to close our eyes again almost as soon as we have opened them and glimpsed the truth. We may all benefit from practising forgiveness. It is quite common for resentments to be nursed against family members and against fellow employees or bosses and former, or even present, friends. It is perhaps even more common to harbour resentment against groups to which we may not belong, such as Travellers, Protestants, Catholics, Moslems, 'Americans', Nigerians and so on.

If the first barrier to forgiveness in such circumstances is a reluctance to name our resentment for what it is, claiming instead that we have 'no problem' with those whom we resent, the second barrier is our sense of righteousness. We (or someone about whom we care) have been wronged, we are convinced, so why should we forgive those who wronged us? This question 'Why should we forgive?' carries much weight, especially when those whom we believe wronged us have neither acknowledged that they did so nor sought our forgiveness. Indeed they may even assert that whatever they did was justified or in our best interests. Or, perhaps, that it was somehow our own fault.

Reasons for attempting to forgive may be explained in terms of self-interest – in other words that it is good for us to forgive – and such reasons shall be considered below. However, there is an even more fundamental reason for forgiving those whom we resent or hate and it is this: forgiveness is a moral and aesthetic act that proclaims us to be human. It is an expression of our highest nature and, therefore, a natural act of completion of our destiny. To assert this is itself an expression of faith in mankind, to believe it is an act of hope and to act on it is a sign of charity. If we forgive minor wrongs, we lay a path for those who approach more grievous offences with trepidation. Nobody can compel us to forgive in our hearts and there is no scientific evidence that we are genetically programmed to choose to forgive. Pure forgiveness is an act of will based on spiritual insight or intuition or principle.

For those with more specific forms of religious faith, acts of forgiveness may be also based on the exhortation of wisdom-teachers such as the Buddha or Jesus. The latter bid us to 'love one another as I have loved you' and such love may be taken to include forgiveness. To obey this exhortation is, of course, not entirely selfless, as those who do so expect a reward in a later life. For people who lack confidence in any argument for forgiveness that is based on pure will or religious teachings, there are other more practical and manifestly selfish reasons for forgiving people. One obvious benefit is therapeutic. If we go around clinging to our resentment and hatred, it can eat us up inside and exhaust our energies, making us bitter and sad to no useful end. We may fear that we shall do ourselves an injustice by forgiving, especially when the wrong that we are convinced has been done to us has not been named by an independent third party or when the person who did such wrong has not been punished in any way. Indeed, the person may even have prospered on the basis of an injustice inflicted upon us. However, even in such circumstances forgiveness releases us from history. In the words of Paul Ricoeur, it 'gives memory a future' by orienting us away from the constant replay of past events that cannot be changed to the consideration of possible actions and development based on what we have learnt from our experience. We may, for example, resolve to devote part of our time to helping others who have suffered worse than us and to assist them in recovering and building new lives.

Those who hear a call to forgive may reject it because they think that they are being asked to 'forgive and forget' and they cannot forget. But forgiveness is not the same as forgetting. In fact, the suppression of memory can be a sign that we have not truly forgiven but have simply attempted to gloss over our pain and hurt. One does not have to be a psychoanalyst to appreciate that such repression may even fuel our resentment in the long term and result in it either imploding and damaging our heart and mind and body or exploding in a rage directed at some third party (perhaps displaced at some unfortunate family member who takes the brunt of our rage at being unable to hurt the person who we believe originally hurt us). Forgiveness can only give memory a future when we have not forgotten the basis for that forgiveness. It is partly because we harbour resentment from the past that we have something to forgive. Forgiveness does not depend on either our forgetting or another person seeking forgiveness. Clearly it is easiest to forgive when someone comes to us and admits that he or she wronged us and is genuinely sorry. It is harder when the person just says sorry but raises suspicions that he or she is doing so largely to avoid further consequences or just to look or feel good. It is hardest of all when they are unrepentant and even self-righteous. To forgive people in such circumstances is not necessarily to change one's mind about the unjust nature of their actions, especially if the original actions really were unjust. Nor is it to allow them to escape the normal civil consequences of, say, a crime such as rape or assault. Nor is it to disarm oneself against attempted injustices in the future. We may, and even must, continue to resist evil and injustice while trying to forgive those who commit injustices.

While forgiving, we recognise the facts of past events for what they were and accept that history cannot be changed. But we offer those whom we resent a way forward that frees them from the chains of their memories. In doing so, whether they accept or care about our forgiveness or not, we help to free ourselves from their negative connection with us. There are some meditation exercises that may assist us in forgiving, especially when waves of negative emotion and memory threaten to engulf us and even fan the flames of dormant or repressed hatred and resentment. I am certainly no teacher of such methods but they involve, for example, imagining that one is breathing in as dark smoke the negative emotions of our enemies. These emotions are then transformed into a white light of love that we exhale towards them. This is a visualisation exercise and we are not trying to convince ourselves that such dark smoke actually exists or enters us or is retained within us as a burden in any way. To make this exercise easier we can begin by imagining first that we are helping those who are close to us by exchanging their problems and negativities for the white light of compassion.

Acts of forgiveness, difficult as they may be, do not just free us from futile memories but also release resources that are blocked from us by the wall of our resentment and hatred. These resources are the treasures to which I referred earlier and I shall now give three possible examples of them.

Some people find it hard to forgive a parent for some pain that has been inflicted, perhaps by physical or sexual abuse or by alcoholism or neglect or narrow-minded ignorance. The resentment blinds them to the reality of their own family history and to understanding some of the principal reasons they have come to be where or who they are. It can blind them to the good in many people whose mistakes or acts caused deep resentment but whose acts may have been unrepresentative and contrary to that person's dominant emotions or intentions in respect of us. By choosing to forgive such a parent, living or dead, the child opts to understand formative influences that may span generations and this can enrich the child's own capacity to make correct decisions for the future. People exercising such forgiveness may also discover much about themselves, unleashing a flood of buried memories and insights and seeing themselves in a new light.

Some people greatly resent their former schools, hating particular teachers who were brutal physically or psychologically and who inflicted on pupils the consequences of their own prejudice or laziness or other limitations. To choose to forgive teachers who were brutal or unkind is not to say that they were right but to acknowledge that they were wrong even if they thought otherwise. We now offer them, alive or dead, a better relationship based on mutual respect. Such an act of forgiveness may unblock cultural and social resources that were violently assumed to be theirs by those whom we now forgive, but that never belonged to them.

Similarly, we may lose sight of the massive and varied heritage of Christianity (or religion in general) behind the wall of resentment that many of us in Ireland harbour against an institutional Catholic Church that we now believe let down and sold short what we held dear earlier in life. The sins of the past – such as personal outrages committed by individual priests, nuns and brothers or the arrogant and crass behaviour of the hierarchy – stand in the way of a clear view of the good and beauty that Christianity can represent. Our level of biblical and theological understanding is generally so limited, notwithstanding the fact that the Catholic Church had every opportunity to teach religion maturely in the schools following the second Vatican Council, that it is hard for us to see beyond our disillusion and to discover in a new way the basis of our warm feelings towards Christianity, even when we are inclined to forgive. But, by forgiving, we can reconnect creatively with many dimensions of our heritage and breathe new life into the Christian tradition. This does not stop us from continuing to be offended by new words or actions from Church authorities or from rejecting aspects of the teaching of particular

Churches that we now find preposterous. It does allow us to locate these within a framework that is more constructive and enabling for everyone.

Hatred cuts us off from the complex reality that forms and lies behind those whom we hate. Hatred may even be attractive or pleasant at a certain level. How much easier it is to feel superior to Travellers or Moslems or 'Americans' than to grapple with the fact that they may honestly see things in a way that differs from our own perspective or to accept that we ourselves are sometimes implicated in the circumstances for which we hold others completely responsible. If we are open, we often have useful or good things to learn from the cultures we think we despise.

Forgiveness of an individual or of a group does not require forgetting or pretence. It requires us to acknowledge our feelings and thoughts for what they are but to extend an olive branch of reconciliation to those who we believe have wronged us. If the offending person or group spurns that extended hand, we may go further and 'forgive' them anyway by being willing to reconcile and by trying to appreciate why they may have acted as they did with the best of intentions or why they were tempted into doing wrong. We may also recognise in many cases that a wrong which they did us in the past does not give them power over us now unless we allow it to do so by clinging blindly to our pain and rage. To forgive may not be easy. I have seen people at the Glencree Centre for Peace and Reconciliation struggle to listen to and understand those 'from the other side'. Even as they are generous and forgiving, each can find new and subtler ways of articulating their grievances and self-righteousness. But even attempted forgiveness that is less than perfect can help to create the conditions for personal or political progress where before there was stalemate.

Sometimes when groups that have had their differences manage to appreciate each other in new ways, their very success can become a threat to others. When I attended meetings that involved a group of western Christians engaged in fascinating and fruitful dialogue with Tibetan Buddhists at a place associated with the Buddha in Bihar, India, I found local Hindus highly suspicious: the latter feared that both sides were getting together to plan the conversion of India and to inflict new indignities on the largely Hindu local population. That such a proposition was patently preposterous did not prevent local newspapers from treating it seriously and thus demonstrating people's recurrent capacity to take offence even where none was intended. How much harder it is to come to terms with offence intended. It often struck me when I saw her at Glencree that Una O'Higgins O'Malley had personally managed to do so in a way that set an example of dignity, presence of mind and determination to ensure that the circumstances of similar offences would be less likely to occur in the future. She was an inspiration. Not all of us have such generosity or energy but each of us can try in some small way to increase the level of forgiveness in the world and so help to give our darker memories a brighter future.

Remembering to Begin with Peace

Geraldine Smyth OP

Initium ut esset, creatus est homo, ante quem nemo fuit.

That a beginning might be made, humanity was created, before whom nobody was.

St Augustine, City of God, 12:20

Something that will not acknowledge conclusion
Insists that we forever begin.

Brendan Kennelly[1]

'Why is Ireland so saturated with commemoration?' It was a young German woman who put the question, one of a group of School of Ecumenics students on a field visit to Belfast. During it, they had encountered many aspects of a city emerging from trauma. Belfast is still dominated by grim interfaces in the form of towering dividing walls and menacing murals, flags, memorials, parades. Victims of the Troubles have not yet been properly acknowledged. Belfast (and indeed the island as a whole) is not yet at peace with its past. Evidence abounds of commemoration with no other end in view than to keep the past alive – and this notwithstanding the many individuals and groups who persevere in the work of peacebuilding. Ireland may indeed be characterised by what Todorov terms an 'excess of memory'.[2] But, equally, no cure will be found through an 'excess of forgetting.'[3]

Divided societies do seem to be magnetically drawn into commemoration of what Paul Ricoeur calls 'epoch-making events',[4] often associated with violence and serving to reinforce the community's consciousness of its identity. Commemoration can take many forms. One cannot but be aware of the ways in which public memory has been constructed around particular versions of history or the ideology of nationhood (as, for example, to steer a way forward in the aftermath of the Irish Civil War 1922–1923). Questions then centre upon issues linked to the control and staging of commemorated events, the focus of commemoration (who and what is at the core; who or what peripheral). Issues about the purpose of commemoration arise (to keep imagination attuned to dead heroes or representations of the enemy, to inspire fidelity to a noble cause or continued grievance against the representative enemy). Commemoration often has a moral purpose, carrying the idea of 'never again' or addressing the aim of recognition of victims and supporting the process of social reintegration.

Clearly in many post-conflict societies, as part of the multi-layered work of peacebuilding, a spectrum of processes linked to memory, truth, justice and reconciliation present themselves.[5] It is not my purpose to rehearse these processes but the argument will be informed by them, though I hold that that healing and reconciliation – and in some instances forgiveness – will not be facilitated by drawing a veil over the untold suffering of victims or denying historical realities of structural injustice or official deception.[6] My intention is to confront the moral and spiritual imperative facing us in Ireland of graciously, painfully laying the past to rest as a *sine qua non* of peacebuilding that concerns us all. I will focus particularly on memory and commemoration in the hope of uncovering the creative relationship between remembrance of loss and the hope of newness. Others have provided a more thorough analysis of commemoration in Northern Ireland – examining its meaning, forms, purposes, applying a phenomenological, historical or sociological lens and taking account of international experiences and analysis. I commend two recent papers on this theme.[7]

Commemoration is part of our being. The sites of memory, whether in the soul's landscape or in the terrain of history, can be deeply evocative cognitively and emotionally. Memory can conjure up, filter and highlight associations of security and joy or of confusion and hurt. Memory can also play tricks with truth, shining a beam backwards in soft or sharp focus, reinvigorating fantasies of harmony or struggles to break free. It can bolster a sense of inclusion or exclusion, even as it forges a causeway inwards and downwards. But memory is about more than reminiscence. Thus writers since ancient times have attributed a moral function to remembering. Insofar as we remember reflectively, we can learn from failures or the encounter with limits, open to different levels of the self or a different view of life. Memory moves the capacity to contemplation. As it weaves the strands of a personal story into some larger narrative, remembering expands the horizon of meaning, giving depth and texture to one's experience of believing and belonging. Memory also integrates us and locates us, enabling a person to feel more at home in a precarious world yet restless for what might be. Someone once said that civilisation began with cemeteries. There it is in a nutshell, notwithstanding the opining of Freud on the matter of civilisation and its discontents.

There is then a way of remembering that betokens civility and indeed humanity. There is, doubtless, unhelpful commemoration, the kind that seeks to stop time or enshrine ideology and power. One such takes the form of monumentalisation. Simply to walk around Belfast City Hall (or certain public buildings in Dublin) is to encounter monuments in surprising numbers – to military regiments, captains of industry or certain political leaders – and is to realise how, on a day-to-day basis, despite their eminent posture and elevated positioning, these figures largely escape notice. Heroism and triumph set in stone to impose a message to future generations. Yet there is almost a pathetic air about their fixed gaze of moral worthiness as passers-by hurry on regardless. The intended connection has failed and, for the most part, these monuments are for contemporary generations as self-importantly relevant as Ozymandias.

I met something similar visiting Argentina in the late 1980s when it was emerging from the era of a brutal security state. On street corner after street corner, such monuments stolidly stood, mutely at odds with the life-concerns of so many oppressed and dispossessed people all around. But I also encountered in the centre of Buenos Aires the group of Madres de la Plaza de Mayo – that living tableau of commemoration that drew others in and conveyed a message to the whole world. These mothers and grandmothers vulnerably holding weatherworn photographs of their loved ones who had been 'disappeared' by the old regime signified an authentically indomitable quality. Their courage was its own monument. In defiance of official denial, their collective presence insisted that their daughters and sons were once living and had left their trace as a sign of the life they had lived among us. Although their trace was physically lost, this act of commemorative witness reforged the broken link between memory and hope.[8]

In Northern Ireland, where a divided people is emerging from prolonged violence, the besetting temptation is to remember not wisely but too well the chosen traumas and chosen glories of their own community, culture or Church. Here the prospect of making peace with the past is difficult and astringent. When considering commemoration, and especially when it is a case of memorialising grievous loss, one must be ready to accept that a pain too deep for tears or even a preternatural anger may be provoked. Such anguished memories are not biddable to the conscious mind. Many who have thus suffered and longed to forget remain haunted by overpowering images of terror and upsurges of grief, blame and desire for retaliation. Survivors of war or violent abuse in the process of therapy discover that their bodies hold memories even after conscious awareness of them fades.[9] The art of remembering well means moving beyond the operations of mind and will and letting go to a shifting, subjective emotional field.[10] In these circumstances, such axioms as whether to 'forgive and forget' or 'remember and forgive' may bypass the sense of abandonment and betrayal. It is not simply about choice. It is no easy matter to reconnect remembering with life rather than death or being ready to 'remember' and include perpetrators of grievous hurt into a community restored to new life.[11] Christian faith here poses a challenge and a paradox. Commemoration is both a mandate and a gift open to all, at once costly and free of charge.[12] It is no accident that the Christian mystery of salvation as announced by Jesus is couched in the symbolic language of remembering. The mandate 'Do this in memory of me' is to be no dead letter but a living word and life-giving event. His followers are invited into this same movement of self-giving – sharing bread and wine, pouring themselves out on behalf of others – 'for the forgiveness of sin'. The hints of something more than human are here. Such generosity breaks open the normative bounds of one's known community, a grace that both integrates and transcends human minds and hearts. Whatever its moral potential, forgiveness is irreducible to moral demand. Gabriel Daly's insistence that human forgiveness is a participation in God's transcendence, a work of grace, always more than the capacity of the will, is fundamental.[13]

Undoubtedly some have experienced in acts of remembrance and acknowledgement a restoring of relationship truth, forgiveness and justice. This seemed to be the aim of the *Facing the Truth* (2006) TV docu-drama which brought together perpetrators and victims of particular atrocities in Northern Ireland. While the intentions may have been good, the prevailing impulse seemed to be directed towards a dramatic spectacle of forgiveness and reconciliation: victims and perpetrators on show, viewers assigned the role of detached voyeurs. But truth is more than the simple negotiation between conflicting memories and forensic evidence, forgiveness more than a trade-off with confession. It is all too common to fix attention on the bereaved in isolation. Conversely there is a responsibility for others in society to acknowledge their part in the rupture and ensuing alienation and to become participants in the process of healing through remembering. Here social consciousness becomes social conscience, involving all in the public mourning that is necessary in post-conflict societies. It has been largely ignored. Una O'Higgins O'Malley indicated possible ways of addressing this collective responsibility in terms of 'the necessity for some structured way of together remembering, expressing sorrow for, and maybe even repenting of, the violence of our shared past'.[14] While hesitant to make an imposition of repentance for acts committed by others, she nonetheless avows that 'insofar as we have overlooked the anguish of the other side and failed to attempt reconciliation with them, we do have matters to repent'.[15]

Already, over the years, particular personal and collective rituals of mourning have taken place. Many have stood amid the bomb debris of McGurk's bar in 1972, Frizell's Fish Shop in the Shankill Road in November 1993 or Omagh's town centre in August 1998, numbed, bewildered. Many have been present at gravesides and darkened churches for remembrance services. Who knows the extent of the comfort or challenge engendered at such rituals? I believe that they did make a difference and that whatever form such ritual takes – gathering in silence, candle-light processions, writing and carrying forward the names of loved ones, symbolic planting of bulbs, listening to a word of scriptural comfort, offering up of prayer – such liturgical actions opened up an otherwise missing space where communities could acknowledge their loss, invoke Christ's presence and promise, and give some awkward shape to solidarity across a rift. They also drew people down into the heartbrokenness of faith and for many a tenuous connection was disclosed between human abjection and the psalmist's lamentation. Rachel was heard again, weeping for her children, refusing to be comforted because they were no more (Mt 2:18). Christ's shout against abandonment before surrendering his life into his Father's hands revealed his total at-oneness with this particular place of desolation (Mk 15:34). Such symbolic shared events paradoxically provided a clearing in which healing through remembering became real and people helped one another to find light in the heart of darkness.

Some have followed where organisations such as WAVE led the way[16] – devising simple human actions and processes of attending to individual victims and survivors of violence and trauma irrespective of creed or politics. Others focus attention on people in particular sectors – RUC widows and orphans, for example. Some aim at support or redress or truth recovery, while other such groups have a therapeutic focus. There is still mourning to be done – in solidarity with victims and survivors in whatever quarter. This will involve an admission of a collective failure and the directing of public commitment to work towards a future of justice, peace and interdependent life. Freud distinguished mourning and melancholia. Others such as John Bowlby[17] have amplified understanding of the power of mourning to enable intense grieving over the lost one towards gradual accommodation to the altered state and a rebuilding of hope. In the task of making peace with the past, everyone is called to mindfulness, called to shoulder something of the burden of responsibility and to reach out in hope of such transformation. In Northern Ireland, it is necessary to rediscover the integral relationship between mourning and renewed life, mourning that offers a time-space for withdrawal and lament and rituals that hold life in fragile trust. Mourning is about surviving into a new day – *sur-vivre* – to go on living through the loss, no longer as hapless victim, not defined by death but by life. Paul Ricoeur speaks analogously of the 'work of remembering' (in preference to 'duty of remembering', which so easily becomes a wheel of no release).[18] This invites into an alternative way of remembering that releases images of possibility in the present and future. It is to this invitation and responsibility towards future life that I now turn.

It is surely time now to mitigate the fixation of commemoration upon death and mortality and to affirm its connection with life and birth. In the dark Autumn days of 1993, following the ghastly killings of those having a quiet Hallowe'en drink in Greysteel, of workers at the city council depot in Belfast and the World Cup supporters watching TV in a Loughinisland pub, something shifted in the public soul. The expressions of outrage across society transcended the wonted rhetoric of condemnation. There was evidence of a nascent solidarity with one another on the basis of ordinary humanity and desire for life expressed in a determination to make a break for the future. This movement had the feel of a life force. Particularly notable was that in the ensuing island-wide rallies, organised by coalitions that included trade union movements, Churches, voluntary bodies, the media and politicians, the appeals for an end of killing and commitment to shared life were expressed in repeated references to a different future for the sake of our children. It became a litany, as if in a newfound conscientious need to bear witness to 'the next generation … for the sake of life'.[19] The ceasefires were declared about nine months later.

While it may not have ushered in the end of violence, this new social consciousness became an unstoppable conviction that peace was coming to birth. And those same motifs of 'birth', 'the children' and 'new life' continued to make themselves heard and felt at further crisis moments, most poignantly in 1998 when three young brothers – Richard, Mark and Jason Quinn – were burned to death in an attack on their Ballymoney home (sparked off by the violence that erupted at Drumcree when police blocked an Orange parade from going through a nationalist locality); and a short time later when Omagh town centre was devastated by car bombs laid by dissident republicans, so many of the victims were children, including a mother and her unborn twins. I suggest that this highlighting in public discourse of the needs of children and of the next generation, in a significant turn of language and imagination, represented a new awakening to the primacy of life over death and of peace over violence. This may seem by the way or even sentimental exaggeration (since it is now known that talks between the IRA and the British government were already underway). And yet, it can be argued that peace needed to be conceived in an imaginary that went beyond calls for 'an end to violence and death'. At this time, a vision of peace was taking shape that went beyond the admissions, finally, that the war was unwinnable and compromises must be negotiated. Certainly there was all of that – in the talk about talks and the choreography of conflict mediation over parades and decommissioning of weapons, with demands over dates and deadlines couched in epithets of who must jump first and which side could claim the moral high ground. But more profoundly, it was as if memory was finding ways to reconnect with imagination, envisioning peace as an alternative way of life for the next generation. Fresh debate was generated about the possibility of shared relationships and social flourishing for everyone's children and grandchildren. Noticeably, while some murals portrayed images of dying hunger strikers and others paramilitaries in battle-gear, underwritten by chilling captions, a new kind of urban art appeared featuring scenes of carefree children playing under trees in the sunshine, as if in aspiration of springtime innocence. Edenesque? Perhaps. But these depictions tapped into a mythology of peaceable life, echoing the symbolism of the tree of life and the healing of the nations represented in the Book of Revelation (22:2). It is unlikely that the artist was making any deliberate allusion, but the imagery of a new heaven and a new earth, of open doors and of the recovery of lost childhood, presaged the change that was in the air. It is worth delving more deeply into the significance of this symbolic discourse of birth and new life as a key to the fullness of peace and to do so in a hopeful correlation between a new social and theological vision.

Julia Kristeva has posited the idea of motherhood and birth as an emblem of resistance to all totalising impositions on another of one's own identity, driven by an inexorable 'fight to the death'. 'Maternal time' for Kristeva asserts the alternative hope of different identities not merely coexisting but in relationship. Birth (and by implication 'maternal time') involves a willing suffering of a rupture at the core of one's body for the sake of allowing the new life of 'an other'. It opens a door to the way to a more differentiated identity and a fuller form of relationship.[20] Although writing in the context of refiguring a new generation of feminism (beyond mimetic rivalry with the masculine world), what is more relevant here is her adducing of birth as a symbol of radical peace with its inclusive, reconciling vision of self and other. The reality of birth is a letting go to new life and an invitation to love 'an other' in attentiveness and self-forgetfulness.[21] In theological terms, this brings us into the realm of creation and of God's providential plan to draw human creatures into that creative purpose in a freedom and intimacy that constitutes a relationship of dynamic life and love. Too often the Christian theology of creation – particularly in its singular favouring of the *ex nihilo* doctrine – aims to protect the sense of God's mysterious freedom and, by extension, safeguards against the idea of the cosmos as site of any pre-existing violent conflict (as in the Babylonian Enuma Elish myth). Theologically important as this is, the idea of creation out of nothing needs to be kept in tensile relationship with the idea of *creatio continua*, with its assurance of the dynamic rhythm of God's constant creative Spirit at work in the cosmos. This is beautifully evoked by the psalmist – with no loss to divine mystery and transcendence: 'When thou hidest thy face, they are dismayed; when thou takest away their breath, they die and return to their dust. When thou sendest forth thy spirit, they are created; and thou renewest the face of the ground' (Ps 104:29–30).

Similarly, the Jewish symbol structure of the Sabbath, with its inherent rhythm of creative work and rest, of humanity's contemplative praise before the marvels of God's boundless goodness, manages to hold together this double perspective. There is a Jewish reading of Genesis 2:3, which links this creative tension with the understanding of humankind as co-creators (Eastern Orthodox would prefer 'co-workers'): 'God rested from all his work that God had created to make.' The paradox here is that God has at once completed the work of creation and allowed room for humanity to create it still further.[22] Thus the Creator God is mysteriously other and graciously a part of our life on earth. Hannah Arendt, secular Jew that she was, writing about the violence inherent in totalitarian systems, posits the idea of natality as more fundamental to our humanity than the defining notion of mortality and as the ground of possibility of all new beginnings.[23] Natality is offered as the creative starting point of peace, newness and conviviality – rather than violence and the overcoming of violence as the determinative framework, which operates by reinscribing death and mortality in human awareness and action. With natality as the point of departure, one can freely imagine radical alternatives to coercion and death-dealing totalitarianism. Because, as Arendt argues, with each birth 'something uniquely new comes into the world',[24] the capacity to think and act new beginnings, even in the face of intended extermination, exemplifies a hope that is ineradicable. Natality thus has the capacity to ground human thinking in respect for the unique and irreplaceable value of every concrete human life in relation to every other unique and irreplaceable life. Natality insists on the possibility of beginning afresh, of asserting the primacy of life and of acting in new ways.[25] It is thus the basis of ethical freedom and of political action. By putting birth and natality into a place of pre-eminence rather than violent struggle, Arendt moves the focus away from abstractions and theoretical justifications for (or even against) violence and expresses attitudes of concern for people's lives concretely embodied and historically situated in equality, justice, diversity and interdependence. Each person is construed as uniquely individual and relational, affected by daily needs, sufferings and joys, given to remembering and oriented to hope and newness.

Arendt's warnings about the attempts of totalitarian powers to eliminate not alone its victims but even the memory of their existence have relevance beyond National Socialism.[26]

The implications for enabling commemoration in Ireland to open up life and peace surely become clearer in this light. For Arendt, and for us, every human life 'between birth and death can eventually be told as a story' so that history itself becomes 'the storybook of mankind'.[27] So too for those concerned to bear witness to the 3,720 victims of Northern Ireland's conflict, and to acknowledge the suffering of the 47,000 people who were seriously wounded, commemoration is a moral act.[28] In this light, commemoration becomes a refusal to consign these lived lives to 'holes of oblivion' as if they had never existed and were of no consequence in the context of some greater scheme of things. Marianne Elliott's recent study highlights the vein of august sacrifice and necrophilia pervading the rhetoric that was constructed around the memory of Robert Emmet.[29] Its cult of sacrifice shaped militant republicanism throughout the nineteenth century and characterised the religious blood mysticism of Pearse's utterances. It is visible too in twentieth-century unionist and republican calls to arms.[30] Is it not time to shape a rhetoric and a worldview that prizes natality and love of life? Such a rhetoric and worldview would nurture the roots of life and the web of life, enabling people to be in creative relationship with those who have gone before, with those around us – and with those coming after us. It is salutary that the positive signs already noted extend now into loyalist areas in mural affirmations of native writers (C.S. Lewis), sports people (George Best) and peacebuilders (Sadie Patterson)[31] and need to be further amplified beyond neighbourhood interfaces into new civic spaces, festivals, intercommunity conferences and opportunities for shared religious celebrations. What I am pressing for here is a culture and practice of commemoration that has natality at its heart and that affirms the hope of new beginnings. I have argued elsewhere that it would be desirable for the governments of these islands, security services, rival paramilitary groups and any, indeed, who incline selectively to cultivate or repress the memory of these lived and living lives to acknowledge that inclusive commemoration is an obligation of human decency and a *sine qua non* of healing, justice and a hospitable future.[32] It would also be salutary for those in positions of Christian leadership to facilitate shared commemorations in witness to a common faith in the Creator God and in the Risen Christ and in the Spirit who unifies divided communities and makes of them a new creation.

As a number of neuralgic centenary commemorations approach – the signing of the Solemn League and Covenant in 2012, the Declaration of Independence in 2016 – is it not timely for political and Church leaders to give consideration together as to how these events might be celebrated, not in ways that valorise violence as the condition of a nation's birth and freedom, and not as commemorating the proverbial 'fight to the death', but as moments of birth and signs of New Creation? As groups begin to rethink the meaning of their history, making space for the memories of the other, it is not too much to hope that they will also rise to commemorating these occasions as 'lifelines' of the future. These 'lifelines' might take the form of shared educational initiatives, research scholarships, interchurch study programmes or youth activities and hospitality programmes for immigrants, sponsored perhaps by the Church fora that have been steadily increasing in the North. We need rituals, spaces, activities, artistic events and musical expressions that leave behind paradigms of trauma and exclusion and evoke longings for healing, willingness to make a new start and courage to cross thresholds in Church and society. God knows what hidden vitality might be released in our church life, worship and witness, as Churches make moves to allow salvation to be seen and touched and felt, less through a forensic approach to sin and being made at rights with God, in favour of images and actions that are signs of the reconciling Spirit at work in New Creation. Such enigmatic gospel words as those about the need to be 'born from above ... born of the Spirit' (Jn 3-8) invite our contemplation so they can speak to our condition, here, now, and reawaken our sense of being called to the fullness of life. The kindred spirit that unites Arendt's natality and the Christian Feast of the Nativity is discernible to those open to the signs of the times. Interchurch peace-walks, initiatives of justice in support of homeless people, for example, or traditional carol services are increasingly a seasonal feature in many places.

These, at their best, give expression to an ecumenism of life, often reflecting a depth of scriptural preparation and shared faith rooted in the capacity of all human hearts to be moved by the promise of birth and the desire for peace and good will to all (Lk 2:14). Such opportunities of grace are redolent with possibilities of a more profound understanding of our context and of this new moment in history. As we open to these together in the light of Jesus' birth into our world of suffering, flesh, limitation – 'born of a woman, so that we might receive adoption as children' (Gal 4:4-5) – who can imagine the splendour of the revelation of God's glory that will appear in our midst in the human community fully alive?

Following this signal, Churches could well take a fresh ecumenical look at the sacrament of baptism in the context of interchurch families. They might reflect (for the first time?) on how they might re-receive the ecumenical understanding of baptism expressed in *The Lima Document on Baptism, Eucharist and Ministry* (1982) as a God-given opening for witness together to the gift of new life, to the liberating power of the Spirit's grace and to the forever new hope in Christ of reconciliation, our sectarian history notwithstanding.[33] By drawing out the meaning both for the child (or adult) and for the welcoming Church community of the baptismal symbols of the water that cleanses and the oil that anoints and heals, Christian community would intensify the common bond of baptism. It would also strengthen belief in baptismal grace as always available to the whole community of believers, most especially at times when the community is in sore need of healing and of reconciliation.[34]

There is a wonderful sense of baptismal newness in an ancient liturgical text for the Feast of the Nativity, instinct with the heartbeat of 'natality' alive in the baptismal community, promising New Creation for all. It is from a sermon of St Leo the Great and still down the centuries its power to exhilarate is scarcely rivalled:

> This is the day our Saviour was born; what a joy for us, my beloved! This is no season for sadness, this, the birthday of Life – the Life which annihilates the fear of death, and engenders joy …

Nobody is an outsider to this happiness. The same cause for joy is common to all, for as our Lord found nobody free from guilt when he came to bring an end to death and to sin, so he came with redemption for all … Let the saint rejoice … let the sinner be filled with joy … let the Gentile be emboldened, for he is called to life …

My beloved, let us offer thanksgiving to God the Father, through his Son, in the Holy Spirit. In the great mercy with which he loved us, he had pity on us, and 'in giving life to Christ, gave life to us too, when we were dead through sin', so that in him we might be a new creation, a new work of his hands …

O Christians, be aware of your nobility – it is God's own nature that you share …

Through the sacrament of baptism you have been made a temple of the Spirit.[35]

This indeed is commemoration but oriented to new birth and saturated with life and hope.

In the week after Christmas 2006, RTÉ screened a programme on the life of Una O'Higgins O'Malley to commemorate her first anniversary. Unaware of this (busy upstairs completing this contribution), I was called down in time only to hear her closing sentence: 'And the "indomitable Irishry" should gaze into the faces of their children, and not their ancestors, when planning for the future.'[36] It was as uncannily apt to the season of the Nativity as it was a crystal summation of her lifework. This hope for the flourishing of peace recalls a poem by Michael Longley with similar echoes of children and Christmas and I wish to conclude with it. Aptly entitled 'All of These People', it likewise intimates the kinship between birth and death and peace that can survive even assassination and robs death of the last word. It centres on two shopkeepers, victims of sectarian killings while they went about their business. Longley remembers them making their living through decent human exchange. He refuses to define them by their deaths but by the vital civility of their daily commerce. It should be quoted in full, therefore, precisely because they deserve to be remembered in the detail of their lives as ordinary peaceful people whose memory is renewed by their innate capacity to inspire peacefulness in others:

> Who was it who suggested that the opposite of war
> Is not so much peace as civilisation? He knew
> Our assassinated Catholic greengrocer who died
> At Christmas in the arms of our Methodist minister,
> And our ice-cream man whose continuing requiem
> Is the twenty-one flavours children have by heart.
> Our cobbler mends shoes for everybody; our butcher
> Blends into his best sausages leeks, garlic, honey;
> Our cornershop sells everything from bread to kindling.
> Who can bring peace to people who are not civilised?
> All of these people, alive or dead, are civilised.

The qualities of peace are not quenched by death. The surrounding images of human compassion defying the sectarian norm are linked by the colloquial Northern 'our'; thus, every character is claimed by the poet, members of one shared community: '*Our* assassinated Catholic greengrocer' is cradled in the arms of '*our* Methodist minister'. And there will be a 'continuing requiem' to '*our* ice-cream man' in the children's chanting by heart of his 'twenty-one flavours'. The continuities of civil society and community will be sustained by those who live on, somehow giving assurance that peace will outlive the war and civilisation repair itself through the free and open human exchange ('Our cobbler mends shoes for everybody', 'our butcher', 'our cornershop').

This community of commerce and the abundance of natural imagery (leeks, garlic, honey, bread and kindling) stand as emblems not alone of sustainment and flourishing, but also of the profound human wisdom described by the biblical author as 'a reflection of the eternal light, untarnished mirror of God's active power' (Wis 7:26). Remembering calls forth hope. For wisdom, we are told, 'makes all things new. In each generation she passes into holy souls; she makes them friends of God and prophets' (7:27).

Notes

1   Brendan Kennelly, 'Begin', *Selected Poems,* New York, Dutton and Co. Inc., 1972, pp. 42–3.

2   Tzvetan Todorov, *Hope and Memory*, London, Atlantic Books, 2003, p. xv. The baleful effect of cultural amnesia is also the burden of Seamus Deane's novel *Reading in the Dark*, London, Jonathan Cape, 1996. The anonymous narrator presents his childhood recollection of a family secret, associated with his disappeared uncle, and his own boyhood attempt to 'read' the meaning of conversations interrupted or photographs kept hidden. Later it becomes clear that his uncle had been in the British Army. In the 1950s that would have been a dangerous memory for a nationalist to acknowledge. It was a memory with which many Irish families identified. It is only since the 1990s that the moral challenge to remember has begun to be publicly acknowledged – in ecumenical services in Dublin cathedrals (attended by the president) and most recently with Alex Maskey (first Sinn Féin mayor of Belfast) laying a wreath at the central War Memorial in Belfast in 2003 and the first government-sponsored commemoration service for the ninth anniversary of the Somme at Islandbridge, Dublin, 2006.

3   Paul Ricoeur, *Memory, History, Forgetting*, trans. Kathleen Blamey and David Pellauer, Chicago, Chicago University Press, 2004, p. xv. In a more narrative mode, Geiko Müller-Fahrenholz describes an encounter with a passing local woman while visiting Ireland who, on seeing him explore a ruined church, pointed back to it, avowing, 'That's what Cromwell did to us', with a fervour suggesting this had happened just yesterday. 'Deep Remembering: the Art of Forgiveness', unpublished paper, presented in Corrymeela, Annual Ministry Conference, 1997.

4   Paul Ricoeur, *Time and Narrative*, Vol. 3, trans. Kathleen Blamey and David Pellauer, Chicago, Chicago University Press, 1988, p. 187.

5   Healing Through Remembering is one such broad-based organisation with members from diverse sectors and political backgrounds. It was established following a visit, in 1999, and report of South African Methodist minister

Alex Boraine on the needs of victims of the conflict in and about the Troubles (*All Truth is Bitter*, Belfast, HTR, 2001) that identified several broad areas for further research and consultation (for example, truth recovery and acknowledgement, story-telling, a day of reflection, network of commemoration, a living museum), all relating to prevention of further violence, the needs of victims and social healing. These areas continue to be addressed via sponsored consultation, dialogue and research. Research papers include Kieran McEvoy, *Making Peace with the Past*, Belfast, HTR, 2006 (also available in PDF from www.healingthroughremembering.org).

6   Geraldine Smyth and Stephen Graham, 'Forgiveness, Reconciliation and Justice', ninth in a series of fourteen papers in *Forgiveness: Thinking Biblically – Building Peace*, Belfast, ECONI, 2002–2003.

7   Healing Through Remembering, Sub-group on Commemoration, papers by John Nagle and by Sheila Fitzgerald presented at HTR Roundtable on Commemoration, Belfast, 19 January 2007, www.healingthroughremembering. org.

8   See Paul Ricoeur, *Time and Narrative*, op. cit., pp. 116–26. Here Ricoeur avows two perspectives on history, reminding us of the 'trace' of a life as not reducible material fact – however necessary this task of historical documentation. But he also intimates the transcending value that '[taking] account of the surplus of meaning "within-time-ness" brings to historicality' (p. 122); see also Geraldine Smyth, 'A Habitable Grief: Forgiveness and Reconciliation for a People Divided' in *Milltown Studies: Essays in Honour of Michael Hurley S.J., Ecumenist*, No. 53 (2004), pp. 94–130.

9   Judith Lewis Herman, *Trauma and Recovery: The Aftermath of Violence – from Domestic Violence to Political Terror*, New York, Basic Books, 1992, Chapter 9.

10 See Mary Warnock, *Imagination and Time*, Oxford, Blackwell Publishers, 1994. She observes that 'our memory, while indissolubly involved in our present perceptions … is also linked, with equal strength, to our emotions'. Thus memory 'can give rise to deep feelings of joy, or of remorse or regret, or simple nostalgia' (p. 110).

11 See Todorov, *Hope and Memory*, pp. 142–7.

12 Miroslav Volf, *Free of Charge: Giving and Forgiving in a Culture Stripped of Grace*, Michigan, Zondervan, 2005.

13 Gabriel Daly, 'Forgiveness and Community' in Alan D. Falconer and Joseph Liechty (eds), *Reconciling Memories*, Dublin, Columba Press, 1998, pp. 195–215. Daly demonstrates from a theological perspective that 'there is something inescapably "religious" about forgiveness' (p. 200) and, in soteriological terms, that '[h]uman forgiveness is an analogical mimesis of divine forgiveness' (p. 201).

14 Una O'Higgins O'Malley, letter to *The Irish Times*, 11 December 1997.

15   Ibid. The author goes on to make a plea *inter alia* for cross-party support for 'a special inclusion in the Remembrance Service held annually at Kilmainham in July of prayers for forgiveness and healing of the Civil War', concluding that 'it would be good to address this unfinished business before the end of the century and the start of a new millennium' cited in *Remembrance and Forgetting: Building a Future in Northern Ireland*, Belfast, Interchurch Group on Faith and Politics, 1998, pp. 12–13. Una O'Higgins O'Malley was earlier a member of the Faith and Politics Group.

16   WAVE Trauma Centre (originally an acronym for Women Against Violence Empower), formed in Belfast in the mid-1990s to befriend families bereaved through violence, has now expanded in scope and location and conducts various projects on the healing of personal and intergenerational trauma, via counselling, artwork and educational and training processes. See also *Every Picture Tells a Story – Dedicated to Children Everywhere*, Belfast, WAVE, 2003, which gathers the stories, art and poetry of seventy young people, aged five to twenty-five, which lay bare something of the untold pain of having lost a family member through violent attack.

17   See John Bowlby's trilogy on attachment and loss, especially Vol. 3, *Loss: Sadness and Depression,* London, Pimlico Press, 1998; first published by The Hogarth Press and the Institute of Psychoanalysis, London, 1980, pp. 23–37, 65.

18   Paul Ricoeur, *Memory, History, Forgetting*, pp. 87. Intent on 'divesting memory of its function of being the birthplace of history to become one of its provinces', Ricoeur does acknowledge the importance of historians' 'sitting down to work' in the archives, though he also insists on the overarching importance of 'testimony' (p. 147). Although not spelled out here, clearly implied is the need for a living connection between memory and imagination.

19   See Mary Warnock, *Imagination and Time,* Oxford, Blackwell, 1994, especially pp. 152–8, on the relatively recent philosophical attention to the idea of moral obligation to unseen others and on subsequent generations. The author argues cogently here against Derek Parfit's claim that such a moral intuition is philosophically incoherent. For a further discussion on intergenerational moral obligation, see also Rachel Muers, 'Pushing the Limit: Theology and Responsibility to Future Generations' in *Studies in Christian Ethics*, Vol. 16, No. 2, 2003, pp. 36–51, 41.

20   See Julia Kristeva, 'Maternal Time' in *Toril Moi, A Kristeva Reader,* New York, Columbia University Press, 1986, pp. 187–213, 206, 209; also Geraldine Smyth, 'Sabbath and Jubilee' in Hans Ucko (ed.), *The Jublilee Challenge: Utopia or Possibility,* Geneva, WCC, 1997, pp. 59–76.

21 See Geraldine Smyth, 'Sabbath and Jubilee', pp. 59–76, where I tease out this association explicitly in relation to the role of women in peacebuilding in Northern Ireland.

22 This links in turn with another Jewish tradition of the *tikkun olam* whereby we are invited to work for 'mending of the world'. Thus in both the Talmudic and Christian traditions, there is an emphasis on human beings as *shutafim* (partners) in the divine work of creation and salvation. See Geraldine Smyth, 'Sabbath and Jubilee', p. 72.

23 More fundamentally for Hannah Arendt, natality (as much as mortality) should be viewed as a primary philosophical category of the human: 'Because he is a beginning, man can begin; to be human and to be free are one and the same. God created man in order to introduce into the world the faculty of beginning: freedom.' Hannah Arendt, *Between Past and Future: Eight Exercises in Political Thought,* Harmondsworth, Penguin, 1977, p. 167.

24 Hannah Arendt, *The Human Condition*, Chicago, University of Chicago Press, 1958, p. 178.

25 Hannah Arendt, *The Life of the Mind: Thinking and Willing*, 2 vols, New York, Harcourt Brace Jovanovitch, 1978. 'This very capacity for beginning is rooted in natality, and by no means in creativity [i.e. in making something out of nothing, rather than out of material embodiment], not in a gift but in the fact that human beings, new men again and again appear in the world by virtue of birth' (Vol. II, p. 84).

26 See Hannah Arendt, *The Origins of Totalitarianism,* third edition, New York, Harcourt, Brace and World, pp. 434–5; also Grace M. Jantzen, *Becoming Divine: Towards a Feminist Theology of Religion,* Manchester, Manchester University Press, 1998, p. 148.

27 Hannah Arendt, *The Human Condition*, p. 97.

28 See David McKittrick, Seamus Kelters, Brian Feeney, Chris Thornton and David McVea (eds), *Lost Lives, Edinburgh and London,* Mainstream Publications, updated edition 2006, extending the first edition (1999) to include those who died in the subsequent years.

29 Marianne Elliott, *Robert Emmet: The Making of a Legend,* London, Profile Books, 2004, pp. 154–9.

30 Ibid., pp. 173–207. Religious legitimisation of sacred violence is evident in the texts both of the Solemn League and Covenant, 1912, and of the Declaration of Independence, 1916; see also Sean Farrell Moran, 'Patrick Pearse and Patriotic Soteriology: The Irish Republican Tradition and the Sanctification of Political Self-Immolation' in Yonah Alexander and Alan O'Day (eds), *The Irish Terrorism Experience*, Aldershot and Dartmouth,

Vermont, Ashgate Publications, 1991; and John Marsden, *Redemption in Irish History*, Dublin, Dominican Publications, 2005, pp. 74–7.

31   Sadie Patterson, the centenary of whose birth was commemorated in 2006 with a conference on peacebuilding and an ecumenical service, was awarded the international Methodist peace medal for purportedly being the first person in Northern Ireland to tell people to stop killing each other. She should also be remembered for her work as a trade unionist and in challenging sectarianism and inequality in the workplace and promoting justice for all.

32   Geraldine Smyth OP, 'A Habitable Grief', pp. 118, 121. My intention here was to contribute to the debate about a truth and reconciliation for Northern Ireland by proposing as an initial step a forum of hearing and healing where victims–survivors would be accorded public space to tell their stories, an exercise that might well have a therapeutic and transformative effect.

33   Section II, 'The Meaning of Baptism', declares it to be 'the sign of new life through Jesus Christ' in a fivefold way: participation in Christ's death and resurrection; conversion, pardoning and cleansing; the gift of the Spirit; incorporation into the body of Christ; and the sign of the Kingdom, while Section III, with equal significance, highlights baptism as 'both God's gift and our human response to that gift'. *Lima Document on Baptism, Eucharist and Ministry, Faith and Order Paper 111*, Geneva, WCC, 1982.

34   Also à propos here is the recent study of the Faith and Order Commission (comprising official representatives of the World Council of Churches and of the Roman Catholic Church), *Participating in God's Mission of Reconciliation: A Resource for Churches in Situations of Conflict, Faith and Order Paper No. 201,* Geneva, WCC, 2006, paras 114–18, where this connection between baptism and 'the divine gift of unity and reconciliation' is made even more explicit. The document cites the Decree of Ecumenism, Vatican II, to good effect – 'Baptism establishes a sacramental bond of unity *among all who are reborn*' (italics mine) – and describes this gift as also 'a challenge to the churches to recognise their accountability to one another, to overcome their divisions', concluding thus: 'The more their unity is manifest, and the more their fellowship flourishes, the more effective the churches' common witness to just reconciliation will be' (para 115).

35   'Sermon I, Nativity, 1–3' as cited in *The Divine Office, The Liturgy of the Hours According to the Roman Rite,* Vol. I, London and Glasgow, Collins, 1974, pp. 185–6.

36   RTÉ 1, *Arts Lives*, 3 January 2007.

With My Missing Hands

Haddon Wilmer

'REMEMBERING TO FORGIVE' is usefully ambiguous. It is commonly taken to mean that forgiving is a kind of remembering. Forgiving does not empty the memory but sorts through the stored-up past to make a hopeful difference to it, even 'healing memories'. Forgiveness transforms what is remembered. It finds its active bodily social form in the present retelling of the past. Think, for example, of old people: they are happy if they can look back on their lives with thanks; they remember to give thanks by telling their story over and over. In order to be grateful, they remember and share memories. Some – most? – people can only remember to give thanks if they remember to forgive: their story only bears telling if it is forgiven. What went wrong will be a source of bitterness, blocking all gratitude and joy, unless it can be told truthfully in a way that forgives, assuages grief, cleanses guilt, brings good out of evil and hope beyond despair and shame. Remembering to forgive achieves forgiveness by the management of memories.

Beyond this, the phrase 'remembering to forgive' has a second meaning. This becomes apparent when we move from gratitude in old people to gratitude in children. Children do not have long memories and they rightly do not spend much energy looking back. They are taught to say 'Thank you' when the occasion calls for it. They must remember to say it until it becomes a polite habit. So too we all need to remember to forgive. To forgive requires a timely decision guided by sensitivity and vision. In situations where forgiving is most needed, it is specially tempting to forget to forgive and then to justify forgetting. Remembering to forgive is difficult; the reminder is needed repeatedly. Remembering to forgive, in this sense, is not a particular telling of a history but a basic readiness of spirit that propels us to experiment with forgiving. Una, as I knew her, was deeply resourced with this readiness to forgive and so as a person she was a clear witness reminding us not to forget to forgive. The two sides of remembering to forgive are needed in practice and one is bound to affect the other.

As the civil war of the 1990s was ending, the Council of Churches in Sierra Leone facilitated reconciliation writers' workshops. From them came a little booklet of poems and prayers, generally short, in simple English and without subtlety.[1] Most are hortatory rather than analytic. One is different: it has gripped me since I first saw it.[2] It pictures forgiving in a succinct drama. It exemplifies both senses of remembering to forgive and reveals both the recreative splendour and the painful precariousness of forgiving. Let us read it line by line.

> O how I loved my hands:
> They were useful to me

Leave aside the rare Narcissus: most people had little chance to see their own faces until silvered glass was mass produced. So each was ignorant of her own face which others scanned and interpreted. A person was dependent on others, whether truthtellers or flatterers, for a sense of what his own face looked like. My face makes me present to the world, but I do not see it. But our hands are different: we see them from babyhood. We play with them, enjoy making funny shapes; we have our fingers talk to each other and learn all sorts of skills with them. By them, we feel and take hold of the world around us. We make friends with them, holding hands; we make enemies, raising our hands against others. The human hand is a prime material condition of human being. Life without hands is hard to imagine: we mostly take them for granted, since they live with us so quietly – until they become arthritic. It is no wonder we love our hands, though there are few poems that say so. We love our hands because they are useful to us. Hands are good for us because they break down the wall we set between the romantic and the utilitarian, between love and usefulness. This is a poem that starts from the good gift of created nature, to be valued and enjoyed.

Today they are no more

A stark line. The hands of this victim of civil war were chopped off. He not only has no hands now but also suffered physically in losing them. People he may have known, or strangers, willed irreparable damage with cruelty and hate and injustice. He has something serious to complain about. There is something to forgive. Perhaps it is too bad to be forgiven.

Wicked man!

So he accuses. He does not say the amputation does not matter. He does not absorb the hurt silently. He resents with pointed denunciation. He does not at this moment remind himself to forgive, though, as we soon discover, he is ready for it. But first this must be said: the word 'forgiving' makes no sense if there is no 'wicked man'. The word contains in itself the recognition of wickedness and wrong. The word 'forgive' does not encourage us to gloss over evil or pretend it is not as grievous as it is. The word 'forgiveness' simply goes on strike and refuses to do any useful work unless we attend to what makes it necessary. It only works when the wickedness or the hurt is noticed and named truthfully – neither exaggerated nor underplayed – and attributed to its true source, not pinned on a scapegoat or nebulous abstractions.

Come and show yourself to me

Restorative justice is so hard because this is its essential requirement: 'Come and show yourself to me.' It demands courage and grace for the victim to issue the invitation and for the miscreant to respond. The invitation is to truth – or at least to come into the place that gives us a sense that we might be coming near the truth even though it may prove to be beyond our grasp. We come into the light not to see but to be seen, to know ourselves to be known without being sure of ourselves. Come: let your guard down. That is frightening. Show yourself to me – who will I see? The man with the machete again? Or a man protecting himself by denying that he ever had a machete? Or a man distraught, who no longer has a self he loves or can pretend to understand? Can he come and show his shame and brokenness? He can bring his body into the light but what 'self' can he show? It may be that others will see he is lost and broken. He will be with others in the truth of his wickedness but his being with others does not achieve a sharing in a common distress and a common comfort. He is shown and shown up. 'Come and show yourself to me' can be an invitation into terror and despair.[3]

Yet in this poem it is, we know, an invitation to forgiveness. The demand, 'Come', is the first step towards forgiving but it brings us to a seesaw, rocking with uncertain balance. Is it accusation or is it forgiving?[4] The uncertainty needs to be sorted. How can that be done? The next line is a clarification but is it enough?

I will forgive you

So the intention is made clear: the forgiver says 'I will forgive' even though I also accuse, 'Wicked man'. Here where the wrong is named and unforgotten, there is not merely a remembering to forgive but also a professed and timely readiness to forgive. We are reminded here of the importance of willing and choosing to forgive. In forgiving, we do more than passively letting go of resentment; we certainly are far from cultivating a superior indifference to hurt. Forgiving involves taking the initiative in creative action for and with the other. The Christian gospel is plain in its teaching and its spiritual practical training: we are commanded to forgive, so forgiving is not, as is often said nowadays, a personal option. We are committed to forgive because we are forgiven.[5] Forgiving is not achieved by the words 'I will forgive you'. They are an invitation and a promise, vital but insufficient. The tense shows that the forgiving still has to be done. Forgiving is not in the wish or a mere attitude or feeling towards the other. There has to be action that somehow liberates the wrongdoer, enabling the wicked man to turn towards something else, into someone else.

Pray with you …

Pray: so far we have seen only the handless man and the wicked man. They are big enough to fill the picture. But now there is someone else: perhaps on the edge, not seen, not named, but present for both. Victim and perpetrator will not come face to face without protection and without help. They will not confront each other as mere owners of what is in themselves, of their pasts and what they have become. They need not meet as though what they are in themselves defines the situation. They are not in bare, spare, shapeless space. 'I will pray with you' means I will meet you and see you in the grace and hope of God. God defines the place we are in with the freedom of forgiving. God remembers to forgive.

I will pray *with you*. Praying for you can easily pervert into praying against you. Praying for people can be done comfortably in safe remoteness from their distress, where our freedom is unlimited by their confinement. With you carries one into the place of the other. Praying together is not the end, not everything. If it were, we would be denying that the Son of Man has authority on earth to forgive sins and so losing the gospel and human hope.[6] This praying prepares for the next step.

Embrace you
With my missing hands

The image is numinous: *mysterium tremendum*. Forgiving shines forth frighteningly: is it intolerable and unworkable? 'Embrace' enacts the will to forgive.[7] It reveals the enormous generosity of forgiving, the courage for risk, the astonishing potential for turning things round and for bringing good out of evil. At the same time, it keeps us on the see-saw. The wicked man may feel the embrace of missing hands as nothing but the persistence of accusation, the sword of revenge not yet turned away. To be embraced by missing hands may mean nothing but accepting the accusation, in a crushing humiliation and an end of hope. The wicked man is condemned by being caught in a dead end. Life does not blossom out into wide places. Rather, it is closed down in the embrace of the missing hands, the hands I took. I am gripped in the uselessness I made when I took the useful hands. I am bereft of the love that was intrinsic to the hands I violated. I am embraced into exclusion.

Forgiving is very fragile, very hard to give, to receive, to believe and to achieve. The man without hands may be tempted to find closure in this fruitless triumph over the wicked man. That was all Nietzsche could see in forgiveness. But the man without hands is not permitted to settle the affair in this way. He has said, I will forgive you, pray for you: so now he must find a way to make this embrace with missing hands genuinely forgiving. Somehow he needs to bring the see-saw between forgiving and accusing decisively down on the side of forgiving.

The Christian story suggests that God embraces us with missing hands and more. We are forgiven by God in Christ the crucified. The wounded hands and the broken body and the blood shed is what God has to give in taking away our sin and forgiving us. The Christian story, from the beginning and now more than ever, was therefore seen to have the potential to incite and justify vengeance against those who could be accused of responsibility for the death of Christ. This potential has been realised not only in anti-semitism, but also in various forms of systematic punitive misanthropy based on the true doctrine of the universality and seriousness of sin. The Christian story is gospel (good news) when it is told as the working out of God's 'Come and show yourself: I will forgive you'[8] but in many tellings it is not gospel. It is rather the pronouncement of condemnation upon the wicked, the unbelieving, the outsiders. So work has always to be done on the telling of the story so that, in its totality, including its practical effects in life, the 'I will forgive you' that God speaks in it comes true fully and finally. In the history of Christianity, we see that critical and constructive argument about the doctrine and theories of atonement have been one way of attending to this task. Any theory of atonement may be assessed by the way in which it makes clear that the 'missing hands' of God in Christ realise and communicate real forgiving rather than some vengeful alternative. Some theories fail adequately to consider the weight of sin – in effect, they miss out the missing hands and heal the wound lightly; others make so much of the wickedness revealed in the killing of Jesus that forgiving is shut down. The work to be done in ensuring that the 'I will forgive you' at the heart of Christian faith and life is not stifled in practice, is not to be left to the theorists of atonement or to other elites. It falls to ordinary people who in various ways have to respond to hurt and loss with whatever capacity they have. We could add to Paul's catalogue of gifts in Romans 12:4-8 that whatever gift we have is to be used to the full. If we have no more than missing hands, then let them be deployed in forgiving. Like Jacob, left by his struggle with the angel to limp through life, we meet life with missing hands if that is what we are left with. Can the embrace we then offer communicate forgiving rather than accusation?

The forgiver, whether God or human, can only give the wrongdoer what he has and can only act with what he has been given, including what he has been given in the suffering of wickedness. If he has lost his hands, he must act with missing hands. But if he has lost his hands, he is not compelled to be vengeful: he may through it all find his way to the generosity and earthed creativity that forgives. He can only embrace with missing hands, but as he does so, he can say again: 'This means I will forgive you. I know the accusation in the embodied memory of my missing hands. I see how it disconcerts and frightens you. I do not discount how it shakes and destroys you, wicked man. I come into that disturbance and fear with you and I share my life and hope with you. I pray here with you. I can and will be friends with you if you let me, but only with missing hands. I give you what I have, which includes what I no longer have.'

'But, how,' asks the wicked man, 'can this ever be forgiveness? Where is the release into new life? You hold me in the rotten memory. That may be tolerable for you: it turns your loss into superior victim-virtue. But it is death for me.'

'I will forgive you, pray with you. I can only embrace you with what I am left with. Praying brings us into the freedom of God, draws us towards a future we cannot make if we go our separate ways. Praying on our way together, add your now regretted wickedness to my missing hands.'

I have not been able to find out whether this poem is autobiographical record or an imagined fiction in the first person. If it is the former, it reports a miracle of grace and hope. Forgiveness of this sort is rare. If it is the latter, which I think more likely, it shows how the vision of forgiving often depends on a wider range of actors and enablers than the two prime parties, the wicked man and the unhanded man. The poet, who does nothing in the poem to advertise his intervention, has the vision of forgiving and brings it to concrete expression. He effects the meeting and the conversation that invites people to forgiveness. It is a key part of the ministry of forgiveness to remind us to forgive, to help us to remember to forgive. We need help continually to discern the need and the feasibility of forgiving, to be truthful about its cost and precariousness and yet to be moved to reach for it. The alternative to forgiving is even less attractive: we must love one another or die.

Notes

1   Sahr Kemoore Salia (ed.), *Friends Again, Sierra Leone,* Council of Churches in Sierra Leone, 2000.

2   Edmund Nicol, 'My Missing Hands', Vine Memorial Baptist church, Makeni.

3   For a biblical example of the uncertainty that besets the one coming to show himself, frightened about the reception he will get, consider Jacob's return to Esau, Genesis 32:13-21; 33:1-4. And the prodigal son, Luke 15:11-32. See also K. Barth, *The Germans and Ourselves,* trans. R.G. Smith, London, Nisbet & Co., 1945, pp. 25, 32f, 37, 40. Barth's forgotten unforgettable little pamphlet might serve as the orchestral part of a concerto, with this even smaller poem playing as the solo instrument.

4   M. Volf, *Free of Charge: Giving and Forgiving in a Culture Stripped of Grace,* Grand Rapids, Zondervon, 2005, pp. 166, 170.

5   Mt 5:43-48; 6:7-15; 18:21-35; Eph 4:32.

6   Mk 2:10.

7   M. Volf, *Exclusion and Embrace: A Theological Exploration of Identity, Otherness, and Reconciliation*, Nashville, Abingdon Press, 1996.

8   Is 1:18: 'Come now and let us reason together, says the Lord; though your sins are like scarlet, they shall be as white as wool.'

The Realism of Forgiveness and Its Risks

Enda McDonagh

IN THE DEEPEST LAYERS OF ONE'S BEING there is hurt: hurt inflicted on self by self, hurt inflicted on self by others, leaving aside the totally accidental physical hurt for which no one is responsible and to which the themes of personal or political forgiveness do not directly apply. In conventional discussion the term 'forgiveness' has a soft, weak ring. Only the unforgiving are strong and retaliation is the symbol of that strength. In personal as in political conflict the weakest still go to the wall and the forgiving are readily identified as the weakest. At best they may be regarded as idealistic or innocent of the ways of the world, while their counter-punching counterparts proudly bear the standard of realism. And so it has been in most of our conflict-ridden and war-torn world from Homer's *Iliad* to Kavanagh's *Epic*. As so often, in Flannery O'Connor's phrase, the violent bear it away; forgiveness becomes no more than an illusion and a dangerous, even suicidal one at that, certainly in political contexts.

There are other ways of reading and writing the same history, be it personal or political. The academic adage that history is written by the victors is seldom invoked to challenge a particular victorious interpretation. There are, of course, notable and recurring exceptions – in the context of various Irish conflicts, the slogan that it is not those who can inflict the most (suffering/hurt) who are the ultimate winners but those who can endure the most. This endurance did not, of course, necessarily include forgiveness but forgiveness does require some capacity for endurance, while continued infliction of hurt excludes the exercise of and perhaps the capacity for forgiveness. Unforgiving and unforgiven persons are defective human beings. Although it is not necessarily their fault, they are both lacking in the health and wholeness of integral humanity. This deficiency might seem more obviously culpable in the case of the unforgiving but the unforgiven may also be contributors to their condition in their unwillingness to seek or accept forgiveness. To understand the reality of forgiveness in its realism and its risks, it is important to consider not only its personal dimensions, critical as they are, but also its sociopolitical dimensions, its religious and inter-religious dimensions and, for Christians at least, its eschatological and divine dimensions.

Divine Forgiveness

It may be more interesting and illuminating to begin with divine forgiveness as recorded in the Hebrew and Christian scriptures, not least because of the paradoxes that its various exercises present. The unconditional, free and gracious gift of the loving and all merciful God embodies a demanding call for repentance, return, conversion of mind and heart and lifestyle from the would-be forgiven human sinners, whether individual Israelites, the inhabitants of the particular cities of Tyre and Sidon or the whole people of Israel. The graciousness of the forgiver, indeed the gratuitousness of the actual forgiving, and the demands made of the forgiven may seem an odd, if not contradictory, couple. The contradiction is partly relieved in the case of divine forgiveness by the recognition that the repentance, the human response to the divine offer, is also divine grace and gift. Although, this is more obvious to us through the history of Jesus than through the recorded history of Israel. In Yahweh's fidelity to his promises and in their realisation through Jesus Christ in what Paul describes as New Creation, both the initiative and implementation of the project of forgiveness and salvation belong primarily and finally to the Creator and Redeemer God.

The free availability of such divine forgiveness and at the same time its ultimate costliness is revealed and realised in the ministry, life and death of Jesus Christ. His teaching and exercise of forgiveness at the Sermon on the Mount and his forgiveness of his executioners on the Mount of Golgotha indicate the divine and human price to be paid by the forgiver. The self-emptying into death of the Son of God in forgiving response as way to the New Creation and New Humanity, Pauline parallels (Romans 5) to Genesis 1 and 2, expose the depth of the recipient response called for from the forgiven. The disintegration of creaturely revolt with its matching disintegration of loving Creator on the Cross provides the opening to Resurrection for Jesus, the New Human, and for humanity as the New Creation. Enabled to die with him in repentance and to rise with him in forgiveness, humanity is fully healed, restored, even transformed. The trusting self-humiliation of the forgiving God is the model for repentant and, within its own circle, forgiving humanity.

Human Forgiveness
In the problematic dualities that afflict all human relationships as gift and threat to one another, as companion and competitor, enjoying and resenting, serious offence may be given and taken whoever's the fault. The consequences can reach from the trivial to the lethal with bitter and long-lasting estrangement between individuals, families and neighbours. Within marital and family relationships, in neighbourhoods and in social and charitable organisations, in religious institutions and political parties, the offence and division emerge sometimes in deeply hurtful fashion and the prospects of overcoming them can be very remote.

Forgiveness does not come easily to most human beings, although coexistence short of true forgiveness and real reconciliation can make living together with such difficult differences tolerable for much of the time. There are always notable exceptions, often modelled among Christians on the words and example of Jesus. There were many such during the Northern Ireland killings, although not all were publicly known. The most striking example of that era was probably Gordon Wilson, who held the hand of his dying daughter Marie at the Remembrance Day bombing in Enniskillen in 1987 while forgiving the killers. Una O'Higgins O'Malley spent a lifetime promoting such forgiveness and organised a memorial mass for her father and his killers on the fiftieth anniversary of his murder. For Gordon Wilson and Una O'Higgins O'Malley, their Christian faith played an explicit and acknowledged role, as no doubt it did for the many other forgiving deceased and bereaved in Northern Ireland and around the world. The great twentieth-century apostles of non-violence among the racially excluded and oppressed, Mohandas [Mahatma] Gandhi, Martin Luther King and Nelson Mandela, owed much of their charisma and effectiveness to their ability to forgive their enemies in the Spirit of Jesus. Beyond the world of political violence, in the quarrels and violence that surface in domestic and other small-scale circles, human forgiveness is no less necessary, no less difficult and no less exceptional. The spouses or the brothers or the neighbours or the colleagues who have not spoken for years remain trapped in the unforgiving deep freeze. Appeals simply to Jesus' way is seldom effective in initiating, still less completing, the defrosting process. Human forgiveness may be finally, if anonymously, fuelled by the Spirit of God but the human spirit has its own journey, long or short, to discern and to travel from paralysing resentment and rejection of the offending other to appreciation and acceptance of that other. The process of forgiveness is only completed by the mutual acceptance and appreciation of offender and offended.

In Truth and Justice

In mutual acceptance and appreciation, truth must be acknowledged and justice done, however difficult both these may be for the participants. But it should be a loving truth, a truth discerned in love, the divine love that embraces offender and offended, a comprehensive love that takes account of the inevitable weaknesses and failures on both sides, however blatant in the circumstances those of the primary offender may be. Justice and its doing is no less an essential component of forgiveness but it should be a generous justice as of the forgiving God, where vindictiveness has no place in the mind of the offended and evasion of rightful due is no ambition of the offender. Again, the thrust of forgiveness with its mutual acceptance will make such difficulties much more manageable than, for example, a simple assertion or denial of rights could. At least in that dynamic of forgiveness and repentance the deeper capacity of each party is called into play and their deeper and more holistic relationship is realised. It is in the healed and fuller relationships of the forgiving and the forgiven that the new and richer realism is achieved, if never perfectly, as against the seriously defective realism of continuing enmity and bitterness.

Social and Political Forgiveness

So much that is spoken and written of forgiveness focuses on one-to-one personal relationships. With all its attendant difficulties for forgiver and forgiven, often of social and political background as already indicated, personal forgiveness can and does work – but not always, of course. Between social and political groups the difficulties increase to such a degree that they become for many protagonists and commentators of a different kind, so that these no longer wish to speak of forgiveness at all. This would appear to be confirmed by the frequently frozen character of group hurt, resentment, rejection and guilt. The ice-breaking that could initiate forgiveness and reconciliation may not be now, or in the foreseeable future, available.

For all the forbidding counter-examples, history does occasionally rhyme with hope of peace, reconciliation, even forgiveness. In the twentieth century, that most destructive of centuries, and in Europe, that most destructive of continents, from the horrors of Auschwitz and Stalingrad, from the rubble of Coventry and Dresden, there emerged a growing integration between the ancient enemies of Western Europe, now balanced precariously in face of the ominous threat of the USSR and its satellites. And then without a shot being fired the great symbolic wall of division in Berlin collapsed and all of Europe was suddenly exposed to the prospects of citizen freedom and inter-nation peace – not all accomplished as yet but so much beyond the hopes of even the most optimistic just twenty years ago. The reconciliation fostered in and by the European Union has had its implicit and explicit forgiving moments and symbols, actions and personalities, as Chancellor Brandt of Germany, for example, sought forgiveness from the Poles and a variety of nations and religions accepted their responsibility for the genocide of the Jews.

In the oft despised continents of Africa and Asia, such insights came earlier in the century and clearer in their intent. Mohandas Gandhi began his nonviolent campaign in South Africa for freedom, justice and peace for its oppressed peoples and by solely nonviolent and peaceful means at the end of the nineteenth century. Through the first half of the twentieth, he developed his political analysis and liberating peace-making techniques in his native India. In theory and practice, Gandhi offered the world ways of political reconciliation and, by implication, forgiveness that have still to be properly recognised and implemented by Western powers. His most significant Western disciple was Martin Luther King, the African American leader of the Civil Rights Movement in the 1950s and 1960s, who, like Gandhi, was assassinated for his efforts. In Africa there emerged the towering figure of Nelson Mandela who, despite universal expectations of a blood-bath in the struggle against the apartheid government of South Africa, enabled a peaceful transition of power. The subsequent Truth and Reconciliation Commission presided over by Mandela's religious associate Archbishop Desmond Tutu, for all the limitations of its achievements, did present a very clear pattern of acknowledgement and confession, repentance and remorse and reconciliation and forgiveness unparalleled in modern politics. Its abuse or evasion by many guilty participants cannot diminish its significance in the development of a politics of reconciliation and forgiveness.

Politics, even in its most secular practices, must eventually acknowledge past destructiveness and those whom it most affected. In the deep heart's core of all civilised relationships between peoples and nations, the need for confession, repentance and forgiveness, however much stripped of their religious overtones, will recur. In 2007, perhaps fresh expressions will help thaw some present frozen connections as well as remembering the need for liberating forgiveness in relation to the slave trade of past centuries and its new manifestations in human trafficking today.

With these African, Asian and African American examples in mind, it is difficult to depress the claims of such forgiving politics to an authentic human reality in their consequences and an authentic human realism in their programmes. Of course, there were risks, as all three examples amply illustrate. But would the alternative of violence and war have posed fewer risks to oppressed and oppressor, their individual lives and community existence? And how realistic would the war alternative have been for the particular oppressed in search of liberation and for the particular oppressors in the longer term? And how authentically and really human would the post-victory and post-defeat relationships have been for the victorious or defeated. In her insights into the futility of such violent military victories and defeats for both sides, Una O'Higgins O'Malley drew together her Irish experience and her Christian faith in ways that were closer to Mandela, King and Gandhi, who also cherished the nonviolent ways of Jesus, than to her patriotic forebears, even her father, whom she rightly cherished so deeply.

By remembering to forgive and forgive and forgive, she helped move Irish people of all persuasions towards being a forgiving and a forgiven people.

Ceasefire

Michael Longley

I
Put in mind of his own father and moved to tears
Achilles took him by the hand and pushed the old king
Gently away, but Priam curled up at his feet and
Wept with him until their sadness filled the building.

II
Taking Hector's corpse into his own hands Achilles
Made sure it was washed and, for the old king's sake,
Laid out in uniform, ready for Priam to carry
Wrapped like a present home to Troy at daybreak.

III
When they had eaten together, it pleased them both
To stare at each other's beauty as lovers might,
Achilles built like a god, Priam good-looking still
And full of conversation, who earlier had sighed:

IV
'I get down on my knees and do what must be done
And kiss Achilles' hand, the killer of my son.'

PART IV

RECREATING

Just God

Una O'Higgins O'Malley

When someone speaks of God I like to hear,
God in the spare no-thingness of the deity, I mean,
not efforts to define, control, explain
and not the endless news of the footsoldiers,
their tireless networkings and holy undertakings,
Just God around, within, both them and me,
God in the quiet of a smile, a tear,
God in the freedom of abstractions,
in the silent grief of elephants over a dead companion
and in the buzzing of a sultry bee.

Resurrection

Padraig J. Daly

There will be a day in the end
When there will be no need
To explain anything,

When we will row
Across the short channel
To the island

And find You standing
Where the white shingle
Drops steeply into sea,

Waiting to gather us
Under Your russet coat.

Funeral Tribute

21 December 2005

Kevin O'Malley

Reverend Fathers and Sisters, Ladies and Gentlemen

On behalf of my father and all my family I would like to thank each and every one of you for being here today. You do us great honour as we gather to celebrate Una's life. Many of you will know that earlier this year Una was very unwell and we feared that she might not survive. However, with the help of the nursing and medical staffs of Beaumont and St Vincent's Hospital she made a great recovery to the extent that last Saturday she was driving and shopping on her own. On Sunday, however, she pulled a fast one on us and this time she had set things up properly for her departure. To begin with, she slipped away quietly in her sleep with no fuss whatsoever. Then followed a remarkable series of circumstances. Her ever-so-caring G.P., Dr Brigid Sheehy, was immediately available. When I phoned Fanagan's Undertakers the telephone was picked up by my good friend Alan Fanagan. When we contacted *The Irish Times*, a further friend Willie Clingan was the editor on duty. And, most importantly, my mother's great friend, Fr Enda McDonagh, was also immediately available to participate in the church services. Enda, you spoke so beautifully last night, and again today – many thanks.

So what was Una waiting for? In our house we believe she was going nowhere until Peter proposed to our Catherine and that occurred very recently. In many ways it was a special drawing to a close of a special life. Given that both her father and grandfather had been killed, it was not surprising that she would develop an extraordinary sense of family. That she would develop a lasting and devoted bond to her sister Maev might have been predictable. That she would cherish and nurture her own family was equally predictable. But the way she developed a public life based on relentless campaigning for reconciliation was surely unexpected.

It started with Meals on Wheels but then developed to public protests against the IRA, being a founder member of the Glencree Centre for Peace and Reconciliation and standing for the Dáil (as an Independent of course). This progression of activities caused quite a stir and, indeed, my father remarked last night that he got a real fright during the election count as at one stage it looked like she might get in!

Her life was based on love, family and her faith. She was considerate, brave, dignified, elegant, spiritual and generous but, boy, was there steel also. Listen to the end of this poem she wrote assessing the future of Ireland called '20th Century Revisited':

> Maybe this blood-stained century
> now should be granted leave of absence
> or amnestied in mothballs,
> and the indomitable Irishry of North and South
> should gaze into the faces of their children
> and not their ancestors
> while planning for the future.

She was proud of her children and tirelessly promoted each of us with the other, thereby providing the glue needed by every family. She was especially delighted with her eight grandchildren: Joanna and Elizabeth; Fiona and Stephen and Eoin; Grace and Brian and Catherine. She would have been particularly pleased with their performances today. A favourite saying of hers was *Mol an óige agus tiochfaidh siad* and she certainly practised what she preached in that regard. Within my own house she was a particular tower of strength for the two girls and Annemarie.

Finally, of course, the great love of her life was Eoin – her young Lochinvar from the West. Together they provided such an example for all couples of love and respect. As children of this happy union we were much loved and encouraged but also expected to contribute to the world around us. Ironically, most of these words are redundant because, in a sense, Una has written her own elegy. Her autobiography was entitled 'From Pardon to Protest' and I will conclude by reading her poem from which the book gets it title:

From Pardon and From Protest

I am from heads held high, stiff upper lips
and 'the Clan's' affectionate laughter
where the pain was seldom spoken to the children
– and never among the teacups.

I am from Celtic spirals and the unresolved riddles
of twisted serpents scrolled on holy pages
I am from dancing-class and make-believe
and graven plaque on cenotaph unheeded.

I am from motherhood and meetings
and an unrelenting trail of grocery trolleys;
I am from history and politics
and letters to the press and pictures of my father.

I am from lines of pilgrims thumbing beads
upon their journeys,
From surgeon's spattered vests and the near-certainty
of an all-loving Godhead
I am from pardon and from protest and – like the spirals –
I return to where I came from.

Peace

Una O'Higgins O'Malley

Behind locked doors they shared their anguished thoughts
about the crucifixion of their leader
spiked with a complexity of fear, of anger and self-loathing
since only one had not abandoned him.
That upper room spoke its reproaches to them
of broken bread dipped in the wine with him,
of splashing soothing water with the cool care of towels

as he had washed and dried their dusty faltering feet
a few days earlier. What lay ahead?
To follow him they had forsaken everything;
what now remained of former lives
to carry on with?
Mary of Magdala was convinced
that she had spoken with him in the graveyard
another two believed that he had talked with them
while walking to Emmaus.
Supposing it were true what was he thinking
of their own betrayal?

When suddenly he stood there in the midst of them,
smiling, easy, natural, blessing them with peace
and teasing those who thought he was a ghost
by sitting down and eating fish with them

as in the old days. The room again was radiant with joy
while the peace which he had breathed on them
poured oil on smarting wounds, on sickening doubts,
never again to leave them.

Chronology

25 January 1927	Una is born.
10 July 1927	Una's father, Kevin O'Higgins, is assassinated. Her grandfather had already been assassinated in 1922.
Christmas 1930	Una makes her first public appearance, reciting a poem on the Gaiety stage ('When mother has a headache/I'm as quiet as a mouse …').
1940	Una's mother, Brigid (née Cole), marries well-known Dublin solicitor Arthur Cox.
1943	Una transfers from the Convent of the Sacred Heart school in Leeson Street to Mount Anville, where one year later she is made head girl.
8 May 1947	Una's older sister Maev enters the Carmelite Monastery in Blackrock where she is to remain until its closure in 1988. She celebrates her sixtieth anniversary in 2007 in the Kilmacud monastery.

1948	Una works for Fine Gael in the general election campaign but ends her involvement the following year when a Fine Gael-led government introduces the Republic of Ireland Act and withdraws Ireland from the Commonwealth.
October 1952	Una marries Eoin O'Malley, a surgeon from Galway working in the Mater Hospital in Dublin. Eoin is related to prominent figures in the national movement who took the opposing side to Una's father in the civil war.
1954	Michael Kevin, the first of six children, is born.
1961	Una's mother, Brigid, dies.
1964	Una's stepfather, Arthur Cox, now widowed, is ordained a priest and shortly afterwards baptises Iseult, the youngest of Una's six children and only daughter. Arthur dies the following year in a road accident in Zambia, where he had been working alongside Irish Jesuits.
Late 1960s	Una becomes involved in the development of Meals-on-Wheels services in the north inner city and other charitable work.
1972	The 'public' phase of Una's life starts when she participates in a picket of Sinn Féin Kevin Street organised in protest at the Bloody Friday bombings. Her placard states 'You Don't Do This in My Name'.

Arising from the picket, Working for Peace is founded, which is to evolve within two years into the Glencree Centre for Peace and Reconciliation.

1973   With Una's assistance the staff hostel of Irish Ropes in Newbridge is used to give respite to Northern guests from the Troubles. Similar work is to continue at Glencree.

1974   The Glencree centre is founded on the disused site of the old army barracks and reformatory. A money-raising trip to the US sees the establishment with other organisations of the Ireland Fund of America.

Other initiatives around this time in which Una was involved include an interdenominational service to commemorate the victims of the Civil War and a prayer service for peace in Merrion Square Park which attracted twenty thousand people.

1977   Una stands in the general election as an independent candidate in protest at the brutality of the so-called Heavy Gang within the Garda Siochana, the police force founded by her father. She polls very respectably in Dun Laoghaire, the same constituency as the taoiseach of the day, Liam Cosgrave, who is re-elected with a reduced vote. (In 2005, although long retired, Liam Cosgrave was present to greet Una's family on the sad occasion of her removal service.)

Una subsequently becomes involved with organisations such as the Irish Council for Civil Liberties, Co-Operation North and the Irish Association.

1979   Pope John Paul II visits Ireland. Una helps organise a vigil for peace in St Patrick's Cathedral in Dublin out of concern that the official programme for the visit contains no interdenominational religious event.

The pope does not attend but one year later Una and a Protestant friend from East Belfast meet the pope in Rome and ask him to help establish separate identities for Irishness and Catholicism.

1981   Una attends a public meeting in the Mansion House organised in support of the H-Block hunger strikers. She explains that she could support most of their demands but not all five.

Una also participated around this time in the enquiry into the penal system initiated by the Prisoners' Rights Organisation and chaired by Sean McBride.

1987   To mark the sixtieth anniversary of her father's death, Una organises a memorial mass in Booterstown for her father and the three men who killed him, Tim Coughlan, Archie Doyle and Bill Gannon. She and Bill Gannon's son Roger do a joint interview broadcast by RTÉ.

Subsequent to this, Una continued to be active in Glencree and the Irish Association and was president of each for a time. She also participated in the Inter-Church Group on Faith and Politics.

18 December 2005   Una dies in her sleep at home.